Shelley Katsh
Carol Merle-Fishman

A Fireside Book

Published by Simon & Schuster, Inc.

New York

The Music Within You

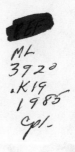
Copyright © 1985 by Shelley Katsh and Carol Merle-Fishman
All rights reserved
including the right of reproduction
in whole or in part in any form
A Fireside Book,
Published by Simon & Schuster, Inc.
Simon & Schuster Building
Rockefeller Center
1230 Avenue of the Americas
New York, New York 10020
FIRESIDE and colophon are registered trademarks of Simon & Schuster, Inc.
Designed by Karolina Harris
Manufactured in the United States of America
10 9 8 7 6 5 4 3 2 1
Library of Congress Cataloging in Publication Data
Katsh, Shelley.
  The music within you.

  "A Fireside book."
  Bibliography: p.
  1. Music, Inflation of.   2. Music—Psychology.
3. Music—Physiological effect.   4. Music therapy.
I. Merle-Fishman, Carol.   II. Title.
ML3920.K19 1985   781'.15   85–10860
ISBN: 0-671-55554-5

Acknowledgments

Many people were helpful in compiling the research and information for this book. We would like to thank Rhonda Brand, Michele Forinash, David Marcus, Joe Nagler, David Ramsay, Steve Schneider, and Caryl-Beth Thomas for the hearty appetite with which they took to the streets and gathered data on music in people's lives. Thanks also to the following musicians who enthusiastically contributed valuable information from their personal and professional experiences: Brad Alexander, Stanley Dorn, Emily Franz, Richard Goldsmith, Barry Greenspon, Carl Gutekunst, John Jake Kella, Ed Lewis, Catherine Roe, Carolyn Snell, Lisa Sokolov, Elizabeth Wolff, and members of the Elusive Quartet, the Manhattan Vocal Ensemble, the Mannes School of Music extension divisions, and the New York Choral Society.

Deepest thanks to our husbands, Jamie Fishman and Mark Gabry, for their enduring love, support, and confidence as we completed this project. It would be difficult to describe in words how much they have contributed to our lives and to this book. Many thanks also to our families and friends for their warmth and love during our months of writing.

The following people have contributed ongoing support as we developed the ideas presented in this book, and have nurtured us through their belief in us and what we have to say: Ken Bruscia, Deborah Chiel, Betts Collett, Richard Erskine, Jonah Gabry, Beth Goldberg, David Gonzales, Jon Kessler, Mary O'Reilly-Knapp, Ilka Peck, Rebecca Trautmann, and the members of the Institute for Integrative Psychotherapy.

Tremendous thanks and gratitude go to Barbara Gess, our editor, for truly understanding the music within us, for using her abundant skills to help us realize our ideas in words, and for having fun with us in the process.

And to Deborah Chiel, thanks for the vision.

Last but not least, we would like to thank each other for the joy and love with which we have created a unique personal and professional relationship.

S.K.
C.M.F.

Dedicated to
keeping the song
of the world
alive

Contents

Introduction   11

I THE MUSIC WITHIN YOU   13
   1 The Natural Role of Music in Your Life   15
   2 Living Rhythms   23
   3 Your Song in the World   31
   4 The Harmony of Life   38
   5 Music in Your Day   42

II FIVE WAYS TO GROW WITH MUSIC   51
   6 Develop Your Creativity with Music   53
   7 Discover Joy Through Music   67
   8 Music for Greater Self-Esteem   78
   9 Building Confidence with Music   87
  10 Music for Closer Communication   95

III MAKING MUSIC: A GUIDE FOR THE ADULT BEGINNER   109
  11 Playing an Instrument   111
  12 Singing Your Heart Out   138

IV LISTENING TO MUSIC: A SPECTRUM OF SOUND   153
  13 Listen to What You Hear   155
  14 Let's Get Physical! Music for the Body   161
  15 What a Feeling! Music for the Emotions   173

16 Mind over Music: Music to Think By   180
17 Sound and Spirit: Music for the Inner Self 189
18 Moving Music from the Background to the
   Foreground   197

V A DEEPER LOOK AT YOURSELF THROUGH SOUND 201
 19 Music Therapy   203

A Final Note   208
Appendix   209
Footnotes   210
Bibliography   219
For Further Reading   224

Introduction

If you were to hear of a source of joy and fulfillment that is accessible to everyone, that can contribute to your emotional and physical health, that can help you become more creative and confident, that can help you communicate more intimately with others, and that is often available free of charge, what would you think?

This source of enrichment is music. Music has served countless functions in the world. It has symbolized countries and cultures in the form of anthems and folk songs, has helped advertisers sell their wares, and has made it easy for lovers to nonverbally communicate their deepest emotions. Believing that music is the best representation of life on earth, scientists have programmed instrumental music into a United States spacecraft in an attempt to communicate with unknown life beyond our earth.

At different times in our history, music was thought to be available only to the very rich, very famous, and very talented. Today, music is available to everyone—as a glorious means of entertainment and a resource of energy, relaxation, and inner growth.

The field of music therapy is devoted to the use of music for creative health. By working with the unique elements of rhythm, melody, and harmony, music therapists help individuals relieve hours of pain, develop stronger bodies, recover from trauma, reduce anxiety, and develop relationships with others.

While music has been used successfully for treating the emotionally and physically disabled, it has been virtually overlooked as a vital source of growth for the healthy individual. While a trained music therapist is needed for the treatment of more serious health problems, anyone and everyone can benefit from the therapeutic nature of music for emotional, physical, intellectual, and spiritual gratification.

If you wake up to music in the morning, listen to music while you do household chores, turn on the radio when you come home from work, or spend evenings in musical exchange with others, you are already using music to enhance your life. Chances are, however, that you have barely scratched the surface of what music can bring you.

This book has been written as a guide for you to realize the abundant resources of music in order to enrich your life. If you have always wanted to play an instrument but felt that you never could, you will learn the simple steps to begin. You will learn how and why to use your voice, the natural instrument with which you were born. We will show you how to use recorded music as a means of energy or relaxation when you need either most. If you have always played and enjoyed music, you may be interested in discovering why your attraction to this art form is so strong. You will learn how to be more creative and more confident, and how to build your self-esteem through joyous, musical discovery.

Whether you have never listened to music or have spent your life on the concert stage, there is something in this book for you. Music is one of life's special gifts. As you read the following chapters, you will discover the music within you and learn how to use this gift to bring you joy and satisfaction throughout your life.

I
The Music Within You

Everything you do is music
and everywhere is the best seat.
—John Cage

1
The Natural Role of Music in Your Life

Music is with us everywhere! We are surrounded by music throughout our lives. In fact, the world over, music is an important part of almost every human activity. Unless you live in isolation, it is practically impossible not to be touched by music coming from radios, televisions, elevators, grocery stores, movies, airports, and just about anywhere. Melody, rhythm, and harmony are with us every day as we are entertained by music, express our religious beliefs through musical prayer, are woken up by our favorite songs, lulled to sleep by soothing melodies, influenced in our choice of beverages by a commercial jingle, and motivated to thin our thighs to a flashy disco beat.

Even when music is not in the forefront of our days, it is constantly in the background of our lives. We are rocked by the rhythmic motion of a commuter train as it punctuates its journey with melodic whistle blasts. We are bombarded by the cacophony of traffic sounds, yet pleased by the melodious talking and laughter of friends at a party. We experience the harmony of a shared moment with a loved one, and the syncopation of our internal daily rhythms against the external rhythms of the changing seasons, days, and passage of time. Practically every aspect of our lives involves music in some way, and rhythm, melody, and harmony, the essential elements of music, are the musical metaphors for our experience.

How often have you heard yourself or a friend say "I'm not in harmony with myself today" or "I've been out of rhythm all week" or "I really feel in sync with that person"? Look at the underlying meaning behind the age-old cliché "We could make beautiful music together." Each of these statements reveals how music helps us understand ourselves and others.

Stop for a moment and think about how you have brought music into your life today. Did you wake up to music this morning? Sing in the shower? Turn on the radio as soon as you got into your car? Stop by the record shop on your lunch break? Listen to an upbeat song to energize your sluggish self? If you find yourself answering yes to most of these questions, have you ever paused and thought about why music is so important in your life? Do you wonder what music is doing for you, or precisely why you prefer the music you do? Would you like to know how you can bring more music into your life? The answers to these questions are simple. Many of them may be found by looking into your development as a listener to and creator of sound and music from conception through childhood. This information will help you understand why music is such a powerful, pleasurable, and universal phenomenon of life.

• Music Before Birth

You know music from your very first stirrings of life. As a pulsation of splitting cells within your mother's body, you are already introduced to the most fundamental and universal aspect of music: rhythm. Within four weeks of conception, your own heart has begun beating, announcing your very existence to the world.

Your days before birth are filled with sound. At this time in your short life, you relate to the world primarily as a listener, with your days as a sound-maker yet to come. To aid you in this task, your ears are fully formed and functioning by birth. Before birth, sound is brought to you through the amniotic fluid and the bones in your head. You are serenaded by vascular pulsations, breath vibrations, and your mother's throbbing heartbeat. You are rocked to the rhythms of walking, running, and even dancing. At times you are jolted by loud sounds from the faraway external world, or soothed by the strains of familiar voices and pleasing melodies. In fact, pregnant women frequently report increased movement of the fetus in response to sounds or music from the outside world.[1]

Within the nurturing, supportive, and growth-inducing environment of the womb, your own rhythms and the sounds around you provide a form of protection, predictability, and sustenance. The constancy of your mother's heartbeat and other bodily pulsations become symbolic sound insurance of your maintenance and survival. This gushing, swishing, noisy place is home, the center of your being. Although it is difficult to know your prenatal experience, it is likely that you came to know these sounds and rhythms as representative of comfort, security, and survival. This idea makes sense when you consider the powerful effect that rhythm, rocking, and soothing tones have on easing the distress of infants and small children. Although rocking and singing to distressed infants is an age-old practice that exists almost everywhere in the world, research has also proven the validity of this method of comforting small children. One study of distressed infants twenty-four to seventy-two hours old demonstrated rocking to be the most effective intervention for comforting, as compared with other interventions that did not include rocking.[2] This study helps explain why the rocking chair is a standard piece of nursery furniture. You may also have noticed your own impulses to rock, hug yourself, or listen to calming music during times of great sadness or distress.

Other evidence of the comfort you once probably received from intrauterine sounds comes from Dr. Lee Salk, who demonstrated that newborns gain weight more rapidly, are less restless, have fewer gastrointestinal upsets, and cry less frequently when they are raised in a nursery in which a tape recording of the rhythmic thump of the adult heart is played continuously.[3] His study suggests that the heartbeat sound provides the infant with a sense of the nurturance, comfort, and security experienced in utero. The presence of these sounds in the new external environment probably ensures the child of continued support and thus promotes positive growth and development. Those who have raised a puppy also know the value of a ticking clock during the puppy's first nights at home. Just as with a new baby, a predictable and steady rhythm seems to provide the puppy with a sense of comfort and eases the transition from mother to a new environment. Clearly, early maternal rhythms provide the first and most enduring experiences of comfort and nurturance. Later in life, the rhythms of music may help re-create these early experiences.

• The Voices and Sounds of Infancy and Childhood

Once you are born, your musical relationship to the world dramatically changes. You now demand the world to listen to you, and introduce yourself as a powerful and often persistent sound-maker. During the first moments of life, your larynx is activated through the onset of breathing. Your first cry heralds your arrival into the world, and is your first statement of self: I am here!

From this moment on, you are a member of the sound-filled world of humankind, a participant in the symphony of life. The sounds you make and those you hear around you compose your very own unique and personal sound history—an auditory painting of all your experiences in the world. You continually create and carry your sound history with you throughout your life. This musical past is revealed in your recognition of a friend's voice, memory of a familiar tune, or recall of the sounds and music of your family.

As an infant, you are just beginning to create your sound history. Since you do not have words to use as a form of contact and communication with others, music becomes one of your primary modes of exchange with others. Through music and sound interaction, you seek to fulfill your needs to be nurtured and related to others. You listen to the melodies of your parents' voices and soon add your own melody to the harmony of the family. You even begin to recognize the difference between your parents' voices, because of your sensitivity to their pitch (high or low quality of sound), timbre (tone quality, such as raspy or husky), rhythm (duration of sounds), and tempo (fast or slow). In fact, research has shown that infants' sensitivity to the music of the voices around them helps them recognize the people in their environment. In one study, four-month-old infants were able to distinguish their parents' voices from those of strangers, just by hearing the voices and without being touched by their parents or seeing their faces.[4] Other studies have shown that infants recognize their mother's voice as early as three weeks of age.[5]

While you were busy listening to the music around you, others were probably listening closely to the music of *your* sounds. The dynamic level (loudness or softness) and pitch of your cries indicated your level of pleasure or distress. These musical sounds helped those around you determine the caretaking you needed. For most of your infancy, your sound-making served a crucial survival function. Once you left the predictable, nourishing environment of the womb, you used sounds to ensure that your basic physiological needs would be met. Peter Ostwald, a musician and psychiatrist who has extensively studied human sound-making, writes:

> Infant screams are remarkably efficient sound signals. . . . Unlike open mouths, wet diapers and other visible signs of baby needs, screams cannot be ignored by averting the eyes or closing a door. Thus, most mothers learn to differentiate sounds which indicate that the baby is hungry, cold, lonely or in distress.[6]

During infancy, sound-making was a creative way for you to evoke a caretaking response in others. During this process, you relied upon the inherent capacity of the human organism to be aroused by sound. This ability is evidenced early in life by the startle responses of infants and newborns.

As adults, many people continue to be aroused by sounds in many different ways. You may wake up to an alarm clock, jump at the sound of a loud or unexpected noise, or pull your car to the side of the road in response to a siren. The stimulating nature of sound, and your willingness to be so aroused, is also behind many of your responses to music. For example, you hear music and are stimulated to tap your foot, sing along, do your exercises, or finish your housework.

The capacity to use sounds to arouse others remains with you throughout your life. When you make sounds, you take action to fulfill your needs for contact and communication with others. The ability to effectively express your needs, wants, desires, and experience of life and to be heard by others is at the core of healthy emotional and physical development. As Ostwald eloquently states:

> No person can live in isolation from others. Sound is an all-important medium for breaking through one's shell to make contact with people. From birth to death the individual screams, gasps, rattles and calls in order to let others know where he is and what he is doing.[7]

Once you are heard and responded to during infancy, the path becomes clear for you to hear and respond to others. This call and response is the basis of all human communication. Listening to and playing music are two examples of how you continue this crucial aspect of life as an adult—hearing and being heard. As Ostwald notes:

> Being listened to is one of the most rewarding experiences a human being can have. Communication with sounds, which starts in the earliest relationship between the newborn and its mother, is basic for emotional empathy. Before words ever come into play, each personality experiences the give and take of communication with tones, rhythms and melody fragments.[8]

One of the most important and satisfying times during infancy is the musical give and take, or call and response, that occurs between mother and child. This early process of reciprocal sound-making is at the core of healthy, nurturing relationships and provides the foundation for a lifetime of satisfying communication with others. Not only do infant sounds arouse a caretaking response, they also invite others to make sounds. Rarely do mothers attend to their infant's needs without cooing, talking, singing, or imitating the infant's own sounds. This, in turn, frequently arouses the infant to make more sounds, which are often further expressions of pleasure about the interpersonal contact.

Once begun, musical, rhythmic sound games may continue for many minutes, satisfying infant needs for stimulation, learning, and the acknowledgment of his or her being. Both physiological and emotional needs are met through collaborative sound-making. Both the production and reception of sounds stimulate the body. The lungs, vocal chords, mouth, tongue, and breath are activated when making sounds. The ears are stimulated, as well as the desire to look and move around, touch and be touched. Emotionally, the reflection of your sounds by another is an important acknowledgment and affirmation of your being. When infant sounds are reflected and imitated by others, feelings of worth, acceptance, and caring are evoked, leading the way to healthy development.

• Satisfying Your Sound Needs

As an adult, you may listen to or use music to continue meeting the sound needs you began in infancy. Music often satisfies the hunger for stimulation, communication, and playful contact with the world. The satisfaction of these emotional needs is as important as the satisfaction of physiological needs.

In a classic study of orphaned, institutionalized infants during World War II, the renowned psychiatrist René Spitz emphasized the importance of stimulation and interpersonal contact during infancy.[9] Of the children he studied, those deprived of the handling, talking to, and play common in normal child-rearing tended to sink into an irreversible decline, which led to disease and even death. These children, lacking opportunities to be held, rocked, listened to, and "sounded" to, clearly lost their will to live. In these cases, the satisfaction of emotional hunger was no less crucial than that of physiological hunger. Thus, early musical dialogue between mother and child, often taken for granted, is actually indispensable to healthy development.

Dr. Eric Berne expanded upon Spitz's work and formulated the concept of stimulus hunger. Stimulus hunger may be understood as the need for physical and emotional intimacy with others, throughout life.[10] In infancy, sound-making is a way of creating such intimacy. Sounds attract others and invite touching, holding, and playful interaction.

As we grow older, opportunities for physical and emotional intimacy often decrease. We learn to limit our touching and holding to a select few, and most of us learn to also refrain from spontaneous sound-making. Many of you have probably experienced the need to hold back in public from crying, laughing, singing, or making other sounds, precisely because the sounds *would* attract attention.

Our craving for music as adults may very well be a way for us to replace our lost spontaneity and freedom for sound-making and touching. Music is a means by which to ward off stimulus hunger and meet our needs for intimacy, comfort, and touch. For example, listening to music is "touching through sound." Think about the last time you listened to a piece of music. Did you feel the vibrations in your body? Did you experience a sense of relaxation or excitation? Were you inspired to sing along, tap your feet, or make eye contact with another person? Were you pleasantly lost in the music? These are all examples of how the music may have touched you through your body.

When you listen to or play music, your emotions and thoughts are also touched. A familiar love song may rekindle memories of a broken relationship; a nursery rhyme, wistful memories of childhood. A commercial jingle reminds you to pick something up for dinner. Music also continually stirs up *new* thoughts and feelings. Think for a moment about your own response to a song or piece of music. When asked what you thought or felt about it, you might choose any of a hundred responses. "I liked it"; "I felt sad"; "I'm thinking about a friend I want to call"; "I'd like to learn how to play that piece"; "I wish I was in love like that"— these are all expressions of how music may touch your thoughts, feelings, memories, and fantasies.

When asked how they use music in their day, people we surveyed frequently reported that they listen to music to keep them company. Clearly music is supplying these people with a touching presence in their lives that satisfies some physical and emotional needs for contact and intimacy. Further, more than half of the instrumentalists and singers we questioned told us that making music provided them with a sense of giving to others. Giving, as well as receiving, is a way to create intimacy and contact with others. In these instances, playing music or singing for others probably served as symbolic touching. In addition, since many of us learned to hold back our natural impulses to make sounds as we grew older, listening to music or creating music through singing or playing an instrument is often a way to satisfy our hunger for sound-making in adulthood.

Although music cannot and should not be used to meet all our needs for contact, closeness, and communication, it is obviously an important source for diminishing stimulus hunger and a way for us to express ourselves and take in support and nurturance from our environment. This is a tradition we learn in infancy and carry with us through our interest in, enthusiasm for, and need for music.

From the very beginning of our existence in the world, music plays a natural role in our lives. Rhythm, melody, and harmony are at the core of our experience of self, communication, and relationship with others. The world of infancy and childhood is filled with music, and it is obvious that we seek ways to continue our musical heritage long after childhood's end. In the next few chapters, we will take a closer look at the meaning and importance of music in our lives, as exemplified through our deep connection to the rhythm, melody, and harmony within and around us.

2

Living Rhythms

A vital element of your musical self that begins early in life is rhythm. During your nine intrauterine months, you were introduced to rhythm through your mother's pumping heart and rhythms of waking, sleeping, eating, walking, and breathing. At the same time, you were also developing your own rhythmic self, and so you experienced two rhythms, your mother's and your own. One author describes this as living in a "floating rhythmic soundworld" composed of sounds from your mother's heart and vessels.[1] Your mother's heart probably beat 70 beats per minute, while your small heart beat 140 beats per minute.[2] Thus, before birth you had already experienced what it is like to match your beat against another's.

To gain a sense of what your early rhythmic world was like, try this brief experiment: tap a steady and comfortable beat on your left knee. Keep that going. Now with your right hand double the beat that your left hand is playing, on your right knee. You will be tapping one beat with your left hand for every two beats that your right hand is playing.

Keep the beats going for a few seconds, close your eyes, and let yourself feel the excitement, stimulation, and security of those rhythms in harmony with each other. You have just created a small musical replica of a part of your intrauterine rhythmic experience!

Once you are born, your natural biological rhythms extend beyond just a heartbeat and begin to have a profound effect on your environment and caretakers. These rhythms are a musical statement of your being, and a great life challenge now awaits you—the creation of a harmonious match between your rhythms and those of others.

Some of us are fast, some of us are slow, and some of us are moderate or varying in our tempo and rhythmic self. Generally, your rhythmic preference is evident within the first months of life and well established by the end of your first year. Dr. Judith Kestenberg, a child psychiatrist, has devoted years of study to the natural rhythms of infants and toddlers, and the interaction of their rhythms within their families and environment. Her observations highlight the importance of respecting a baby's natural rhythms. Responsive, cooperative rhythmic interchange between baby and the environment ensures healthy emotional and physical development.[3]

Just as early sound play leads to effective communication with others, so does early rhythmic meshing lead to satisfying rhythmic relationships with others later in life. Interactions in which an infant's natural rhythmic inclinations are not respected are felt by the infant to be unsatisfying, frustrating, and uncomfortable, and may lead to continued uncomfortable rhythmic interactions throughout life. The early recognition and validation of your unique and personal rhythmic self as it emerged is basic to your emotional and social comfort as an adult. As Kestenberg states: "[Children] function better and enjoy doing things more if they are free to use their originally preferred rhythms."[4] Thus, the rhythmic relationship between a mother and her child is often a precursor of healthy or unhealthy growth and development. A mother's capacity to attune herself to her infant's rhythms, respect her infant's attention-nonattention cycles, and follow her infant's rhythms of sleeping and feeding are crucial for healthy development. When a satisfying blend of mother's and baby's rhythms occurs, rewarding and pleasurable experiences emerge, and a form of silent, reciprocal music is created.

Validation of your early rhythms by those around you was probably not always easy. As an infant, you most likely attempted to impose your natural eating, sleeping, and waking rhythms on your parents. You demanded that your rhythms be accommodated, rather than following the established rhythms of those around you. At times your rhythms may have caused considerable dissonance within your family as your parents' rhythms of waking, sleeping, and eating became disrupted. At other times, your parents may have imposed their rhythms on you, preventing you from lingering sensuously over each bite of food as they rushed off to work or a movie. The reconciliation of these rhythms into a pace comfortable for all was one of your first encounters with the need to blend your music with the music of others. Under the best of circumstances, harmonious coexistence was created. Under poor circumstances, rhythms clashed, melodies were unheard, and the world was experienced as arhythmic, dissonant, and acutely uncomfortable.

Similar rhythmic metaphors probably still exist in your life. Although you need to respect your own rhythms, you also live in a world filled with other people. A harmonious blend of your individual rhythms with others' creates satisfying life experiences. The inability to blend with contrasting or simply differing rhythms creates disharmony and discomfort. An awareness of your areas of rhythmic harmony or disharmony can help you create positive rhythmic relationships with yourself and others, and attain greater fulfillment in your life.

• The Dance of Life

The intertwining of individual rhythms with the rhythms of others has been extensively studied by communications researcher William Condon. Condon believes that much of our experience in the world is based on the rhythmic synchrony within us and between us.[5] "Synchrony" may be understood as the occurrence of more than one rhythm at the same time or rate of speed, as in synchronized movements while dancing or typing or even engaging the clutch on your car. Condon has identified two types of synchrony: self-synchrony and interactional synchrony.

Self-synchrony is the simultaneous occurrence of your own rhythmic patterns in movement, speech, and other body functions. Self-synchrony makes it possible for you to perform many rhythmic actions at once, such as talking, walking, and dancing. Condon's research has also shown that people tend to move their bodies in rhythm with their speech and actually dance in time to their words! A lack of rhythmic integration may appear as the absence of synchrony in a person's movement and speech.

Our perception of synchrony or asynchrony in others is so acute that psychotherapists and doctors often use this as an indicator of the presence of health or disturbance in an individual. For example, asynchronous speech and movement is often a sign of physical or emotional illness. Think back to the last time you had a cold or were experiencing a strong emotion, such as sadness. Your body movements, speech, and other rhythms, such as pulse rate and breathing, probably reflected your emotional or physical state, by either speeding up or slowing down or not matching one another. Another example of a rhythmic mismatch is having your thoughts race ahead while your body says "Stop."

Close friends and family members are often quite sensitive to a change in your natural rhythmic behavior, or self-synchrony, and use this information for clues about your emotional or physical state. You have probably had someone say to you "Wow, you sure are peppy! What happened?" or "You really look and sound down in the dumps." When people make these kinds of comments to you, they are reacting to your rhythms and the other, musical cues in your behavior, such as the pitch of your voice.

Awareness of the integration of your rhythms of movement, speech, breathing, and other body functions can help you synchronize your rhythmic self in order to attain more satisfying and supportive life experiences. A sense of your own synchrony and preferred rhythms is an important way to center and ground yourself. To grasp this idea, take a moment now to get in touch with your rhythmic self:

Exercise 2-1

Find a comfortable sitting or lying position. Put your right hand on your heart and let yourself feel and experience your heartbeat. You may want to close your eyes in order to help yourself fully contact this important basic beat within you.

As you experience your heartbeat, allow yourself to withdraw from the thoughts, demands, experiences, and rhythms of the rest of the world. Let yourself fully contact *you*, without interference from the outside world.

Now begin to pay attention to your breathing. Notice the rhythmic flow of your breathing. You will probably begin to feel more relaxed and more in touch with yourself. Let yourself experience the exquisite natural rhythmic synchrony that nature has created between your breathing and your heartbeat. Relax. Breathe. Feel the integration of these two rhythms. Let yourself enjoy them. They are you! Now gradually let yourself begin to feel and listen to the environment around you. Feel the surface on which you are sitting, and listen to the street sounds outside your window. As you bring yourself back into contact with the external world, see if you can maintain a sense of your rhythmic self.

Sometimes it is easy to lose a sense of your rhythmic synchrony as you become caught up in the hustle and bustle of your life and the demands from the world around you. While growing up, you were increasingly faced with demands from the outside world that often interfered with your natural rhythmic preferences. As a child, you may have been told to hurry up, when your natural inclination was to linger. Or you may have been rhythmically swift in movement and thought, yet slowed down by a family that was slow to think and act. School days, work days, bus schedules, commuter trains, and eventually the rhythms of your own spouse, children, roommates, and co-workers have all influenced your tempo and rhythmic inclinations. Many people faced with the rhythmic mismatches and demands common throughout life begin to hold back their natural rhythmic selves in order to accommodate the external world so they may continue to obtain the love, attention, security, and sense of belonging they require. Yet, a compromise of personal rhythms often brings a loss of self and discomfort at work or in relationships.

It is likely that you have experienced many blendings of your rhythms with others, and have at times either held back your natural rhythms or been pleasantly complemented by the rhythms around you. In these instances of bringing your rhythmic self to the world, interactional synchrony begins. Simply stated, this is the silent dance that occurs between you and others during conversation and other forms of interpersonal interaction. While in conversation, for example, people tend to synchronize their movements with one another, composing a silent duet of mutual recognition and responsiveness. Our inclination toward interactional synchrony begins early in life. Condon's films of infants have demonstrated their natural tendency to move their bodies in rhythm to the speech of the adults around them.[6]

Still, there are times when interactional synchrony does not occur, probably due to significant differences in rhythmic styles. This idea helps explain why you feel good with some people and not so comfortable with others, or "in sync" with some and "not in sync" with others. Mismatches of rhythms are often experienced as minor irritations with the other person involved in the interaction. Often familiar clichés are used to describe these experiences, such as "We make beautiful music together" or "He travels to the beat of a different drum." In either case, you are responding to the music of rhythm. You feel your own rhythms and seek their acceptance and validation through positive and complementary rhythms with others.

An awareness of your preferred rhythmic style can help you adjust, at times, in order to achieve more positive relationships. Sometimes you may choose to be with people whose rhythms are in contrast with your own, so as to achieve better balance and integration. For example, a rhythmically fast person might choose to spend time with someone who is more laid back, in order to relax and slow down at the end of the day. This may also work in the opposite direction, as in spending time with a fast person in order to become energized.

You are influenced not only by the rhythms of other people but also by the rhythms of nature, the universe, your culture, and your physical environment. The rhythmic passage of the seasons, day into night, and movement of the planets and ocean tides all subtly affect your being.

Women in particular are especially attuned to their internal rhythms through their monthly menstrual cycles. Yet, even this cycle is prone to individual idiosyncrasies and patterns. Highlighting the important rhythmic nature of this biological process is the fact that the birth-control method that monitors the monthly cycle is known as the *rhythm* method.

We each have our own internal rhythmic clock, and our waking and sleeping cycles are unique and individual. Some of us are owls, or night people, by nature, and some of us are larks, or morning people. In this regard, the customary nine-to-five work day may not rhythmically suit each of us. Also, changes to a different time zone, as a result of travel, are well known to be disruptive and disorienting to our internal rhythm.

Different cities, cultures, and physical environments also present different rhythms for you to adapt to. New York City and other major metropolitan areas are notorious for their fast pace. Country settings, on the other hand, present slower and more leisurely living rhythms. An awareness of the rhythms of your environment will help you understand your own needs, preferences, and desires in relation to your rhythmic self.

• Rhythmic Reasoning

The music of your rhythms can be a useful tool for achieving success and happiness in your daily interactions. Before taking a major personal or professional step, stop and take a minute to synchronize your thoughts, breathing, and movements. This will add to your sense of confidence and esteem. Once you have done this, allow yourself to be aware of the rhythmic meshing between you and another during an encounter. If you are asking your boss for a raise or a vacation, pay attention to her rhythms of speech and movement. You may wish to accommodate your rhythms by either slowing down or speeding up, in order to achieve a satisfying and complementary interaction. If your boss "feels" good about the conversation with you, it is more likely you will obtain what you are asking for.

Any time you are feeling frazzled, upset, or out of touch with yourself due to the rhythmic pace or demands of your life, use the brief exercise outlined on pages 26–27 as a way to center and ground yourself rhythmically. Becoming more centered with your natural rhythm and synchrony will help you deal more effectively with the demands of the external world.

Music offers many other opportunities for rhythmic centering. When you choose to listen to or make music, it is likely that you are seeking to regulate your rhythmic self. Through your choices of music, you create an opportunity to attain synchrony with yourself and the external world. The next time you sit down to play or listen to music, think about the rhythm and tempo of what you have chosen. There is a reason why you were attracted to that particular record out of your entire record collection. Do you need to slow down, speed up, or stay right where you are? By checking in with your physical, emotional, and rhythmic state, you can begin to find the reasons for your choice and preferences for particular music at particular moments in your life. It is likely that the rhythm and tempo of the music are basic to your choice.

When you listen to or play music, it is also probable that you are providing yourself with rhythmic nurturance, support, and stimulation. As an infant and young child, you were probably regularly rocked and rhythmically bounced. These experiences occurred at times of distress as well as play. When you were uncomfortable, sad, or scared, you were held and comforted. When you were happy, energetic, and playful, you were bounced on someone's knee, swooped up into the air, and joyfully jostled. As you grew older, your opportunities for these kinds of rhythmic interactions probably diminished.

Music and dancing are two options for fulfilling your craving for rhythmic interaction with the world. Listening to a slow symphonic piece of music may provide you with the sensation of being held and rocked. Slow dancing with another person certainly fulfills this need. Fast, upbeat music often provides a sense of playfulness, energy, and stimulation, just like being bounced as a child.

Your natural rhythms and rhythmic interactions with others occur every moment of your life. Either in or out of your awareness, rhythm subtly affects your sense of who you are and how you function in your relationships. Chances are high that you have used the music of rhythm in your choice of friends, lovers, work environment, home environment, and even career.

Take a closer listen to the music of your rhythms. Did you linger over breakfast, savoring each sip of coffee, or did you dash down a glass of juice on your way out the door? Did you feel yourself rushing ahead of yourself, or did you experience an even integration of your thoughts, movements, and accomplishments? How have your rhythms blended with your environment and other people? As you waited for the bus or sat stopped in traffic, did you nervously tap your foot, or did you let yourself fantasize about the coming weekend? During your lunch break, did you silently fume as the bank teller seemed to take an excruciatingly long time completing your transactions, or did you pass the time comfortably listening to your "Walkman"? Your answers to questions like these will give you clues about the tempo of your life, and lead you toward more positive rhythmic reasoning with yourself and others.

3

Your Song
in the World

Through your voice, you bring your personal song to the world. Your voice is your own individual melody, another potent statement of your being and the music within you. The development of your song begins quite early, when your birth cry heralds your entrance into a world in which vocal sound-making will be your primary tool of communication. Within your first few years you will move from creative, musical vocalizing to the purposeful use of words for contact with others.

• Beginning Your Song

Your musical vocalizations and babbling begin at three to eight weeks of age and are composed of open vowel sounds, such as "ah" or "oo," often referred to as "cooing."[1] During your first month you explore your vocal possibilities and become oriented to the human voice. In direct contrast to your crying, which is often loud and harsh at this stage of life, you also begin humming, which is usually an expression of pleasurable feelings.

In your second through sixth month, the amount of your sound-making increases, and you add more dimension, variety, and intention to your melody. You begin to experience "vocal contagion," which is the process of being stimulated to make sounds by the voices and sounds around you. If you have spent time with young infants, you have probably noticed how they tend to babble, sing, and coo in response to mealtime or party conversation. Songs and lullabies specifically directed to the infant also add to vocal contagion. These draw the child's attention to sounds and stimulate his desire to respond to and participate in human communication.

By five months of age you begin to use consonants,[2] which require a more sophisticated use of your tongue and lips than do vowels. Thus you prepare yourself for uttering your first word, usually occuring between six and twelve months of age. During this period, you also demonstrate the ability to repeat tunes, imitate the vocalizations of others, and pick up the particular sounds of your culture and language. Your vocalizations are quite melodic and singsong in quality, and you continue to lay the musical foundation for your melody in the world.[3] Although you are born with the capacity for making all speech sounds, many will not be developed if they are not a part of your native language.

As a toddler, you were probably a free, expressive, and joyous maker of sound. Sound-making was a way to release tension and energy, create a response in others, and entertain yourself. If you were provided with a supportive and encouraging sound environment, the gentle cooing and gurgling of infancy developed into the melodious babbling and raucous vocalizations of toddlerhood. You probably punctuated every life experience with a sound, one minute crying, the next shouting with glee. Sound-making accompanied almost all of your physiological and emotional experiences, as well as growing cognitive abilities. During this time of life, your parents no doubt heard you babbling or singing to yourself in the early-morning hours, during play, or before falling asleep. These sounds were part of your natural inclination to communicate and tell the world how you felt. It is likely that you also frequently invited others to participate in your elaborate sound experiments as you happily squealed, clucked, and hummed.

All of the vocal music of this time in your life was an important part of your language development. The process of forming musical sounds into words usually begins within eight to twenty-four months of age, as part of the natural inclination to communicate fully with others. The first use of words is often met with much anticipation and excitement by parents. Once satisfied to imitate their infant's rhythmic sputtering, they now lavish praise and attention on the infant for his attempts at simple words, such as "mama," "daddy," "bye-bye," and so on. Through this process children learn that their parents' melodies have meaning, as musical phrases become sentences made of words.

Before children understand words, they are listening intently to the melodies and songs of the people around them as a way of understanding the intent of their communications. A toddler may not be able to grasp the literal meaning of the words being spoken by another, but will most likely understand the intent of the words by listening to the music of the speech. A cooing, melodious, soft voice will probably indicate caretaking; a loud, harsh, abrupt voice, annoyance or impatience.

During the second and third year, many children develop the ability to sing and remember songs on their own.[4] This is an important part of healthy emotional development at this stage of life. Marjorie McDonald describes these songs as "transitional tunes."[5] They are songs or lullabies that were probably first sung with mother or father and are now sung by the child alone. Such songs may comfort the child or aid in separating from the family in the same manner as a teddy bear, blanket, or other transitional toy. As adults, we continually remember old and create new transitional melodies or songs, which evoke memories of a particular person, place, and time and help us maintain an attachment to emotionally significant events and people. This may be another explanation for the importance of songs and music throughout our lives.

As children increase their vocabulary, they are encouraged to use more words and fewer musical sounds when communicating their wants and needs. In the transition from music to words, speech is often high-pitched and singsong. This is often a time of conflict, as children begin to feel the push to refine their sound-making into more "grown-up" or "appropriate" expressions. By the time children are four or five years old, many have taken in negative messages about their natural, expressive, musical selves. "Stop whining," "Don't talk like a baby," "Say it like a grown-up" are all common messages children hear about their growing facility with speech. From this, they frequently perceive that there is something wrong with their natural, spontaneous expressions. It is possible that they may begin to hold themselves back even more and attempt to accommodate the grown-ups around them in order to receive the love and attention they desire.

Sometimes the physical environment also affects the development of a child's expressive self. For example, children who grow up on a country farm may be permitted to extend and expand their noisy, musical selves in a way that apartment-bred city children are not. The environment within the home may also have a positive

or negative effect on a child's expressiveness. The arrival of a
new baby or the presence of an overstressed parent are often
causes to tone down a toddler's play and sound-making.

• Song Communication

When you gain language and leave behind the musical sound-
making of your early years, you do not lose the music of your
childhood. Your speech remains fundamentally musical. You develop a special tempo, tone quality, pitch range, and dynamic
level to your voice, which may be considered components of your
individual melody. The musical quality of your voice is a relative
indicator of your age, sex, health, and emotional state. A shrill,
high-pitched, or loud voice may suggest that you are scared or
angry; a soft, melodious, even voice that you are joyous or content.
In these ways and more, you are literally singing when you use
your voice as a means of communicating with others.

Throughout your life, you have learned how to use your melody
in different ways in order to meet different desires and needs.
When you wish to bring somebody close to you, it is more likely
that you will use soft, pleasing voice music rather than distancing
voice music, such as shouting or whining. You also still use music
to help you understand the complete meaning of someone else's
words. To say to someone "You sound angry" or "I hear your
happiness" is to respond to his melody as well as his words. Sometimes the music is more revealing of a person's thoughts and
feelings than his words could ever be. This is why, for example,
you may say to someone "You say you're not sad, but you sure
sound sad." Often the music tells all.

An interesting experiment that will help you detect the music
of language is to listen to someone talk *without* listening to the
words—that is, to pay attention only to her melody.

Note the tempo of her speech, the rise and fall of pitch, and
the number of beats between words and sentences. Treat each
sentence as if it were a musical phrase.

Are the sounds inviting to you, or would you rather be listening
to something else? Do you consider this a dissonant or a harmonious song? Is there too much repetition or too much variety? Do
you feel inclined to turn the volume up or down?

The answers to these questions may tell you why sometimes

you feel strongly attracted or repelled just listening to someone speak. Perhaps you like or do not like that person's song in the world, just as you may like or dislike a particular piece or style of music. Your feeling about a person's melody contributes to your attraction to her or him and is similar in nature to your sense of rhythmic synchrony or asynchrony with another.

• Your Enduring Melody

Your voice is your most sensitive and personal instrument. You probably have very definite ideas and feelings about it, which come to mind while reading this book: "My voice is too low . . . too high . . . too loud . . . too raspy . . . too babyish . . ." and so on. The way you feel about your melody is often a clue to your beliefs about your expressive self.

If you like the way you sound, chances are you feel good about yourself and what you have to say to the world. Since you manipulate your voice music moment by moment, either consciously or unconsciously, it is easy to learn how to be so in control of it as to gain both personally and professionally. In Chapter 12, you will learn how singing may help you naturally change the music in your voice in order to bring a more satisfying personal melody into your life.

In the process of acquiring language skills, we often suppress much of our spontaneous, musical, and expressive self, leading to later discontent with our personal melody. This may be another reason why we need and crave music as adults. When you listen to, sing, or play music, you are once again granted permission to experience the joy of your creative, musical, sound-making self. Even though music does have structure and order to it, the range of sound and expressive possibilities in it far exceeds that which you have in words. You may hear high and low sounds, funny and sad sounds, play fast and slow sounds, loud and soft sounds and choose to listen to or perform any of several kinds of music—classical, jazz, disco, folk, blues, blue-grass, and so on. In these ways, music provides hundreds of expressive experiences, impressions, and meanings.

Playing or listening to music can help you recapture the creative, expressive melody that you may have left behind in early childhood. When you regain this natural and spontaneous part of yourself, you also recapture your natural confidence, creativity, self-esteem, communication, and joy. These five elements of life are your birthright and are crucial for the creation of a happy, successful, intimate, spontaneous, and productive life.

When you listen to or play music today, it is likely that you choose music that complements your own song or brings to life a hidden aspect of your sound self. Music offers an abundance of melodies and sounds, from dissonant to consonant, from exuberant to subdued. When you listen to music, you may select a particular melody that suits your unique emotions, needs, and preferences at any given moment. For example, if you are generally soft-spoken, you may feel tremendously gratified by listening to the loud voice of a rock-and-roll singer. While vicariously singing along, you may realize a hidden part of your expressive self that has been waiting to be released into the world. Or, if you spend much of the day talking, taking charge, and being heard by others, you may choose to end the day by listening to quiet, lyrical melodies as a way to balance out the experiences of your day.

To help you understand how you choose music at different times to complement your own personal song or to realize the parts of your expressive self that are waiting in the wings, think for a moment about the voices you listen to in music. Do you prefer female or male vocalists? Opera or rock singers? Loud or soft singing? How do these voices resonate with your own voice or with the different parts of you? Do they tend to be similar, contrary, or complementary?

In addition to the human voices you listen to in music, think also about the individual voices of the instruments you especially like to hear. How does the voice of a certain instrument complement your own voice, say what you wish you could say or realize a part of your potential? Do you wish to soar like a flute or thunder like a drum? Does a violin solo speak the sentiments you long to sing? Or do the variations of a solo jazz piano express the range, variety, and infinite possibilities that are also you? Perhaps you already use the voices of different instruments as auditory imagery to help you through times of stress. The auditory memory of a triumphant symphony may successfully guide you through a difficult meeting where your ideas are on the line. Or the thought of a sensitive love song may dispel your anger during a disagreement with your spouse. Listening to the human or instrumental voices that attract you may give you clues about yourself—your hopes, dreams, wishes, secret self, or public self.

As you continue to discover the meaning and importance of music in your life, you will learn new ways you can use music to support and express your personal song to the world. Your song is important, unique, and worth being heard!

4

The Harmony
of Life

When you bring your song to the world and join in with others, you create the harmony of life. As you grow from infancy to adulthood, opportunities to experience harmony abound. There is harmony within, as well as outside, you. There is harmony in nature, and harmony in your relationship with others. In fact, the natural order of life seems to encourage harmony through the seeking of peaceful and complementary coexistence among living things. The sun rises and sets and you accommodate your eating, sleeping, and waking cycles to this pattern. The moon rises and the tides go in and out accordingly. The seasons change and you obediently alter your activities and clothing. The planets move rhythmically and predictably through the sky, and somehow never collide, as the earth spins around in orbit among them. Time passes. People grow, work, change, bear children, form relationships, eat, sleep, and eventually pass on all that they are and have learned to others. Although whole in your own life, you are also an important part of what makes up the wholeness of the world. This is the creation of harmony.

Simply described, harmony is a state of agreement and order, or, arrangement of aesthetically pleasing relationships among the elements of a whole. In music, this is the simultaneous combination of tones or sounds, or, hearing more than one note at a time. For example, different instruments in an orchestra playing notes from one piece of music create harmony. In this way, life is also like an orchestra. Like an instrument, you contribute your own individual sound and rhythm as you join with others to create a harmonious melody or song.

There is little question that your original, fundamental experience

of the harmony of life begins first and foremost with yourself—
your body. Your heart pumps a solid and persistent rhythm that
syncopates with your breathing. Blood and other fluids rush
through you as your eyes blink, muscles twitch, and intestines
contract. To these you add your other rhythms of waking, sleeping,
eating, working, and playing. You experience the rise and fall of
thoughts and feelings, which are related to the rhythmic action
of chemicals being released in your brain, and the humming of
messages through your neural pathways. To this already miracu-
lous creation of internal harmony, you add speaking, walking,
singing, writing, dancing, drawing, and hundreds of other activities.

The combination of all of these different parts of you creates
a harmonious person—a unique orchestration of thinking, breathing, and feeling. When you are truly in harmony with yourself,
life can be a joyful, replenishing, exciting, and fulfilling experience,
as exhilarating as hearing the sounds of an orchestra or choir
that is perfectly in tune and in rhythm.

If life is like an orchestra, then our families are like a small
ensemble. Depending on its voices, rhythms, and sounds, the family
may comprise a jazz quartet, a chamber ensemble, or a rock group.
For most families, the birth of an infant requires significant readjust-
ment of the family music group. A new rhythm and song has
entered the scene, which demands to be heard. As this new little
voice is heard and responded to, the song of the family may
change for a time as energy is directed toward the care and nurturing of this new member of the ensemble. During this time, if
their sounds are imitated, their rhythms reflected, and their music
enjoyed, most infants experience life as harmonious and good.

As you pass through infancy, and during most of your growing
years, you become increasingly social, and demands to harmonize
with those around you increase. This means that your needs, wants,
rhythms, sounds, and songs are not always number one on the
hit parade! You must now find new ways to be in the ensemble
of the family and comfortably blend your personal needs and
desires with those of other family members. Sometimes great disharmony results from this process. You want to sing when others
want to be silent. You want to eat when others want to work.
You want to be subdued when others want to be active.

There are many ways in which disharmonies in life may be
resolved, just as a piece of music can be resolved and come to

a comfortable and reasonable close. Much of how adept you are at resolving conflicts is learned from your family. For example, growing up in a family where each person blends melodiously and rhythmically can lead to ease in harmonizing with the world.

Throughout your growing years, you are introduced to an ever-widening circle of people, social experiences, and harmonic possibilities, to which you add your individual musical self. In general, it is safe to say that you probably have sought out peer groups, relationships, and work and social situations in which you may comfortably harmonize and still maintain your unique self. Marriage and other intimate relationships are a prime example of the search for harmony with another. In this way, many seek to be as a duet of two instruments, each holding a solo while also blending and complementing one another.

For most people, harmony is a satisfying, peaceful, and nurturing experience, a state many want to achieve. As the stresses of modern life become more pronounced, personal and interpersonal harmony becomes an increasingly important and valuable commodity. The recent popularity of the self-help field and the rapid rise of the holistic health movement both tell of people's growing desire for harmony in their lives. Fast-paced city living, the cutthroat business world, noise, and pollution all detract from our ability to respect our own natural rhythms and personal song and to attain harmony with ourselves and others.

Music is an abundant source of harmony. Almost all music involves harmony of some kind. Although some music may be purposely dissonant in its harmony, and you may not like the harmony in all of the music you hear, there is harmony nonetheless. Perhaps this is another important reason why people crave and desire music. Music may be a healing and healthful antidote to modern-day tensions and disharmony. In fact, this is an age-old belief. Pythagoras, who extensively studied the interrelationships between mathematics, music, medicine, and astronomy, believed that a daily "dose" of music could lead to greater harmony between a person and the universe.[1]

Through music, it is possible to experience the harmony you may be seeking to create in yourself and in your relationships with others. At times you may wish to experience different kinds of harmonies or blendings, and this will be reflected in your music choices. Sometimes dissonance is appropriate and necessary for consonance to occur, just as an argument or disagreement may be the route to concurrence. Or sometimes you may choose to listen to music that complements your own internal harmony, thus creating a sense of wholeness between yourself and your environment.

It is exciting to know that when you experience harmony in music, you are also experiencing harmony within yourself. By listening to a piece of music that you find particularly harmonious, rhythmic, melodic, or soothing, you will begin to feel soothed, whole, and "in harmony." This is probably the reason why many people do not enjoy listening to atonal or dissonant music, because as they listen, they begin to experience these feelings themselves.

Playing an instrument or singing with other people is another way to experience harmony within yourself and among others. Singers and instrumentalists alike will tell you that there is no more exquisite sensation of harmony than the blending of one's voice or instrument with another's. This is a joy many experience when they sing with other people during social or religious occasions.

To be in harmony is a challenge. On the deepest level, it means maintaining the integrity of your own song and personal rhythm while openly considering and acknowledging all the songs and rhythms around you. You can begin to get a sense of this challenge by listening to the harmonies of your environment—the city you live in, your work place, and your home. What are these sounds, songs, rhythms, and harmonies like? How do the different rhythms and voices blend or clash? How do your voice, natural rhythm, and harmony fit into this soundscape? If you were orchestrating this piece, what would you change, add, or keep the same? What sounds need to be louder, more subdued, more melodious? What would be a blending of instruments or people that would be just right for you?

Just as your song and rhythm are meaningful and worth being heard, so too you are a significant instrument in the harmony of life. Let your song be heard, hear the songs of others, and you will be well on your way to the creation of harmony in your life.

5

Music in
Your Day

We all have music in our day, either in the forefront of our activities or as background to routine chores. Many people use music quite deliberately for specific purposes. A lawyer we .know listens to sixties rock and roll every morning before leaving for work. The music makes him feel good, he says, because it brings to mind pleasant memories of his more carefree teenage years. Thus armed with the energy and a pleasant frame of mind created by the music, he feels prepared to face a long day filled with clients and court appearances. One woman told us that listening to classical music eases the boredom of cooking and helps chores pass quickly.

These are but two of the many ways people use music as part of their day. Many people are so accustomed to music in the background of their day that they are not even aware of its presence and effects upon them. However, one thing is certain: When the music stops, everyone notices!

Music is equally important as a background or accompaniment to work as it is for play and relaxation. Many people use music to help them relax after a long day in the office. Others use it to help stimulate physical activity—as an accompaniment to exercise or dancing, for example. Making music often helps to release pent-up energy that may have built up from sitting in an office or other work environment all day. Certainly we know that the first thing children do during recess is make sound. Perhaps music serves a similar function for many of us when we are "released" from the confines of the work place.

It is no accident that music plays such a central role in our day. We are continually invited to listen to more and more music, and we make it clear that we want music in our lives, as evidenced by the booming record industry, musical birthday cards, our interest in the latest stereo and tape-deck equipment, and our fascination with the top rock stars.

The ways that you can use music in your day are as infinite and creative as your own imagination. There are many opportunities for expanding your musical tastes and knowledge through new music experiences, if you feel that you need and want more music in your day, as did many of the people we surveyed. A greater awareness of how, when, and for what purposes you use music currently will help you determine these needs and wants so that you can compose a personalized daily music program for maximum benefit in your life.

Filling out the checklist below can guide you to new ways to creatively add music to your life.

1. Do you wake up to music?
   __yes   __no
   a. If yes, what type?

   __classical   __hard rock
   __jazz   __ethnic
   __easy listening   __disco
   __soft rock   __other_____
   __country and western

   b. Reason for your choice:

   __relaxing   __keeps me company
   __energizing   __enjoyment
   __sets a mood for the day __other_____

2. Do you listen to music while you are getting ready for work or school?
   __yes   __no
   a. If yes, what type?

   __classical   __hard rock
   __jazz   __ethnic
   __easy listening   __disco
   __soft rock   __other_____
   __country and western

b. Reason for your choice:

__relaxing   __keeps me company

__energizing   __enjoyment

__sets a mood for the day   __other_____

                                    _____

3. Do you listen to music on your way *to* or *from* work or school?

   __yes   __no

   a. If yes, what type?

   __classical   __hard rock

   __jazz   __ethnic

   __easy listening   __disco

   __soft rock   __other_____

   __country and western

   b. Reason for your choice:

   __relaxing   __keeps me company

   __energizing   __takes my mind off the

   __fun   anxieties/concerns of the

   __makes travel less boring   day

   __keeps me awake   __other_____

                                    _____

   c. Means of listening to this music:

   __"Walkman"

   __singing to self

   __car radio

   __hand-held radio

4. Do you listen to music while at work or school?

   __yes   __no

   a. If yes, what type?

   __classical   __hard rock

   __jazz   __ethnic

   __easy listening   __disco

   __soft rock   __other_____

   __country and western

   b. Reason for your choice:

   __relaxing   __keeps me awake

   __energizing   __keeps me company

   __helps me work   __way to socialize with co-

   __makes work less boring   workers

   __makes the day go by faster   __other_____

                                    _____

5. Do you listen to music when you get home from your day?
   __yes   __no
   a. If yes, what type?
   __classical   __hard rock
   __jazz   __ethnic
   __easy listening   __disco
   __soft rock   __other_____
   __country and western
   b. Reason for this choice:
   __relaxing   __keeps me company
   __energizing   __accompaniment to house-
   __takes my mind off the anxi-   hold chores
      eties/concerns of the day   __sets a mood at home
                                  __other_____
                                  _____

6. Do you listen to music before you go to sleep or while falling
   asleep?
   __yes   __no
   a. If yes, what type?
   __classical   __hard rock
   __jazz   __ethnic
   __easy listening   __disco
   __soft rock   __other_____
   __country and western
   b. Reason for your choice:
   __relaxing   __keeps me company
   __sets a mood   __takes my mind off the anxi-
   __comforting   eties/concerns of the day
                                  __other_____
                                  _____

7. Are there other ways that music is a part of your day?
   __yes   __no
   a. If yes, how?
   __accompaniment to exercise
   __practicing an instrument or voice
   __playing music with others
   __dancing to music
   __singing in the shower
   __lunchtime concerts
   __evening concerts

___listening to street music
___sharing music with family (playing or listening)
___other_____

8. Were you aware of the amount of music in your day?
   ___yes   ___no
9. Would you like to have more music in your day?
   ___yes   ___no

• How to Release Your Musical Dreams

We all have a musical dream. Some of us dream of being a flashy rock star; others, the conductor of a great orchestra. Still others feel especially attracted to an instrument and so imagine themselves the master of its particular sound. For example, a businessman we know feels such a great affinity for bagpipes that he stops whatever he is doing when the opportunity to see or hear them arises.

In our surveys about music in people's lives, we found that almost everyone has a musical dream. Over one third of the people we questioned told us they had always wanted to play an instrument, while half said they had at one time wanted to be some kind of musician. In addition, ninety percent told us they wanted to bring more music into their lives, through listening, singing, or playing. These numbers truly sing out the presence of a musical dream in us all.

Whatever your musical dream is, it says something essential about who you are or wish to be. Your musical dream may be a strong indicator of your hopes, fantasies, and perhaps that part of your expressive self that you feel you must keep hidden from the rest of the world. This is often a part of yourself that you think or feel you ought not share with others, or that you simply have never had the opportunity to develop. Frequently the reasons for keeping this part hidden or underdeveloped have to do with your sound-making experiences in infancy and childhood. For example, keeping a lid on in response to messages to not make noise may later be expressed in your holding back what you wish to say, sing, or sound off about. From this suppression may arise a musical fantasy to be a powerful opera singer or a cacophonous drummer.

Just about everyone we interviewed had a music story or dream to tell us. Most expressed the wish for their music experiences to have been supported or continued as a presence in their lives. Below are two exercises geared to help you realize some of your forgotten musical potential, relive your personal musical story, and discover your hidden musical dream. One of them requires only a pencil; the other, your creative imagination.

Exercise 5-1

1. Do you sing?
   __yes   __no
   a. If yes: __only by myself
              __with others
              __by myself and with others
   b. If no, what do you think is the reason?_____
      _____
   c. If no, do you want to sing?
2. Do you play an instrument?
   –yes   __no
   a. If yes, what instrument(s)?_____
   b. If no:
      Have you ever wanted to play an instrument?_____
      Have you always wanted to play an instrument?_____
      Which one(s)?_____
      What kept you from learning?_____
      _____

3. Have you ever wanted to be a musician?
   __yes   __no
   If yes, what kind?_____
4. Do you want to bring more music into your life?
   __yes   __no
   If yes, how?
      __listening
      __playing
      __singing

Exercise 5-2

Find a comfortable position, either sitting or lying down. Let yourself relax, and feel your own rhythm, melody, and harmony.

Once you are relaxed, begin by imagining a place where music is created—a stage, symphony hall, jazz club, or even your own living room. Let your mind rest on the place that you like best.

Imagine now that you are the player. What instrument will you play? Or perhaps you are a singer. Will this be a solo concert, or have you invited others to play along with you? What types of instruments are they playing, and how do they enhance or support the song that you are sharing with the world? What type of music are you playing? Classical? Jazz? Rock? Country and western? Is the music melancholy, cheerful, or varied? Is it dissonant, loud, or soft?

As you continue to imagine yourself playing music in the environment you have created, let yourself hear and see the musical dream that you are releasing. What does this dream say about you, or that part of you that is standing in the wings waiting to be expressed?

You may let your music continue for as long as feels comfortable to you. Then, as you bring your music to a close, check in with yourself. How did you feel releasing that music? What were your thoughts as the music played on? Did you find yourself wanting to hold back, or do even more?

Now that you are more aware of what your musical dream might be, begin to think about your present life. How can you begin to express this dream, or a part of it, by either singing, playing, or listening to music?

• Opening the Doors to Music

For many, the world of music is seen as a closed door, a missed opportunity, or a wistful memory. Contrary to these beliefs, the world of music holds gifts, pleasures, opportunities, and a special place for each of us. Beginning right now, we invite you to open yourself to the world of music. There is enough music to hear, play, and sing for everyone. Whatever your previous musical experiences or lack of them, there are treasures yet to be discovered in you and in the world of music that awaits you.

We invite you to release your musical dream and thereby experience a release and expansion of your emotional, intellectual, spiritual, and expressive self, leading you toward a more fulfilling and satisfying life. A release of your musical dream will also mean recapturing the natural music within you, which once fully existed in your childhood and may have been lost during your growing years.

In the following chapters, we will guide you toward the release of the music within you. For some, this may mean more music listening, to a greater variety of music. For others, it may mean the beginning of study on an instrument, or reviving old skills that have been allowed to lie dormant. Remember, there are enough hows, ways, whys, and whats of music for you to find the musical path that is most satisfying, fulfilling, and beneficial for you.

However you decide to pursue music in your life, know that you *are* music. As the composer John Cage has said: "Everything you do is music and *everywhere* is the best seat."[1] By simply being alive, you are a perpetual and wonderful symphony of sounds and rhythms—an important instrument in the harmony of life!

II
Five Ways to Grow with Music

From the heart it has sprung;
into the heart it shall penetrate.
　　　—Ludwig van Beethoven

6
Develop Your Creativity with Music

Creativity is essential for human health. It is through the creative approach to life that we discover the world around us as infants and learn social skills as children. Think back to when you were a child. . . . You and your friends probably made up games and stories within seconds! Each new situation to a child brings with it a score of possibilities for fun, stimulation, and learning.

Now think of your life as it stands right now. Do your creative thoughts flow freely, helping you to explore new and different options at work? Is your life spontaneous, and open to surprising pleasurable moments? Or do you count the hours at work and come home to the same situation every day, turning to TV for escape?

If your answer to this last question is yes, or if you are feeling stuck, trapped, and unhappy in your life, it is probably owing to the loss of creative power that we so often experience with the "onset" of adulthood. Many of us are under the impression that once we become adults, because there are more responsibilities in our lives, we have to limit our options and be more "serious." This usually means being less playful. Although responsibility is essential in adulthood, the loss of creative power and joy does not have to be a by-product of growing up.

The capacity to be spontaneous, inventive, and inspired is within you, regardless of your age, sex, occupation, and ethnic background. Each human being is heir to a universal creativeness that has little connection with inborn talent. Abraham Maslow, father of humanistic psychology, calls this "primary creativeness." He believes that it comes out of the unconscious and is the source of new discovery, novelty, and ideas that differ from those that exist in the moment.[1] Your dreams are an example of primary creativeness; they are always novel, always new, and always free. They emerge from a wellspring of creativity that is your heritage from birth.

Primary creativeness occurs "in process." This means being involved in the creative moment, abandoning the worries and cares of the day, engaging the creative childlike energy within you. Primary creativeness does not necessarily result in a finished product, such as a completed painting or a musical composition. It is the experience of being alive in the moment and in touch with our natural creative inclinations, as well as being free to respond spontaneously to the environment in a creative manner.

Dancing to music is another example of primary creativeness. When did you last respond to the rhythms and melodies of a favorite piece of music with your body, letting yourself move freely and expressively to the sounds? If you were in a comfortable environment at the time, chances are that it was a joyous experience for you and afterward you felt creative, strong, integrated, and *healthy*. Your feelings were probably reflected in a special glow on your face and a bright sparkle in your eyes. In addition, you probably experienced a more positive sense of your identity as a person. Dr. Rollo May, who has written extensively on the creative process, states: "We express our being by creating. Creativity is a necessary sequel to being."[2] The act of creating in the moment is a way of continuing to create who you are.

Creativity is a gift that enables us to develop new ways to solve problems and meet our needs. It is an essential tool for productive daily existence. There are times, out of necessity, when we call upon our ability to think creatively in order to deal with situations such as a sudden change of plans or a health emergency. At times like these we value our creative ability to come up with new, quick alternatives for action.

When a daily routine or job becomes boring, we need the use of our creative assets. Noted psychiatrist Sylvano Arietti stresses the importance of creativity in liberating the human being from the usual choices of his day. According to Arietti, creativity can also help you develop a positive attitude about yourself and about your work.[3]

On a global level, creativity becomes crucial, as it is the means by which we will unearth safe sources of energy and find new ways for countries to coexist on this planet in a more fruitful manner. The innate creative sense we expressed in the past, when we were young, needs to be nurtured and fostered in the present, for then we can experience richer lives as adults, nurture the creativity of our children, and actively participate in the creation of a more harmonious world.

When we honor the inherent relationship that exists between creativity and psychological health, we open new doors to self-discovery. There *are* ways in which you can become more creative in your life. Music is the most accessible, and certainly one of the most enjoyable.

"Music is the key to mastering the creative process,"[4] says Lorin Hollander, virtuoso pianist, teacher, and music lecturer. Music is a means of reconnecting the forgotten joys of creative living to your present life and of feeling the emotional, social, physical, and intellectual benefits that accompany involvement in the creative process.

Music can help you become more creative in the following ways:

- **Listening.** Listening to music stimulates creative movement and thought and enhances the creative content of other activities.
- **Singing.** Singing is a creative expression in and of itself.
- **Playing.** Learning the skills necessary to play an instrument can help you become more creative at home and at work.
- **Improvising.** By trying your hand (or voice!) at musical improvisation, you'll feel the full extent of your creative capabilities.

• Listening to Music for Creativity

Listening to music is an activity available to everyone. As we listen to music, we submerge ourselves in a creative medium. We listen to creative ideas and sounds, absorb them, and incorporate them into our being. By listening to music, you gather material for your own creative use. For example, you may suddenly find yourself singing a song tomorrow that you enjoyed listening to today. The more listening exposure you have to music, the more material you store in your creative reservoir for future expression.

Active listening stimulates our creative energies. In Chapter 1 you learned about the essential role of call and response in early development, which is our natural inclination to respond to sound with sound. This is one reason why it is so difficult to resist singing along with a familiar tune. When we hear a melody we know, we often begin singing it without thinking. When we listen to music, we are naturally drawn into the creative process. Many people who would ordinarily not allow themselves to sing, for fear of embarrassment or rejection, will give themselves permission to do so if they are singing along with recorded or live music. Our appetite for creativity becomes stimulated by the familiar melodies, and we satisfy this hunger by joining our creative sounds with those of the musical environment.

Follow your inclinations to sing along with music as you listen. Your desire to do so is natural, and the creative release is important for your full emotional health. It doesn't matter what type of quality your voice has, or if you can sing in tune. (Active listening and singing along with music can actually help you learn to sing in tune.) What matters is allowing yourself to participate in the inviting creative process that listening to music provides.

Our physical creative energies are also triggered by music listening. Try sitting perfectly still while listening to a very rhythmic piece of music. What happens? Most people find it extremely hard to keep their feet from tapping in time to the music. Certain types of music impel action. A prime example is rock and roll. This music provided permission and motivation for self-expression, contributing to the social upheaval of the fifties and sixties. Because it taps into our inborn desire to respond to rhythm, rock and roll probably *is* "here to stay." Similarly, the dance music chosen for social gatherings is often seen as being responsible for "making or breaking the party." The right music can coax closet dancers out onto the dance floor, bringing movement and life to the occasion.

As a way to discover more of the creative energies in your body, find a place to let your body do what it naturally knows how to do in response to music: move. Here are some suggestions:

Exercise 6-1

When you are home alone, put on some music that fits your mood at the moment. Most people know instinctively what would feel right to them. As a key, listen to your inner rhythms. Are you feeling highly energized, or are you tired and moving rather slowly? Find a piece of music that sounds the way your rhythms feel.

Either sit, lie down, or stand, and listen to the music as it surrounds you. Let your body move the way it wants to. Allow yourself to be as creative as you like during these private moments. Take up as much or as little space as you need to express yourself.

Become part of the rhythm of the music, using your hands and feet to create sound. Blend with the melodies you hear by using your voice. Hum, or sing "Ah" if you don't know the words. Probably much of your day is spent conforming to the rhythms of others. Let yourself celebrate your own rhythms and melodies now, as you feel yourself in creative harmony with yourself and with the environment.

Try this exercise with different types of music and/or at different times of day. Give yourself permission to reconnect with the natural creativity inside your body.

Exercise 6-2

Go dancing with someone you like and trust. Feel the live energy of the room and the excitement and sheer fun of sharing music and creative movement with others. If you are just beginning to let yourself sing, this is a good place to practice using your voice. The music will probably be loud enough for you to feel safe.

Exercise 6-3

The next time you are at a party where there is dancing, join in! Be aware of the music and the way your body wants to move. Don't fight your natural creative flow as the rhythms, melodies, and harmonies touch you.

• Music for Your Creative Mind

Music is inspirational in nature. Melodies conjure up images and memories and can trigger our imagination. In order to experience the creative and imaginative powers of your mind as it is influenced by music, try this experiment.

Exercise 6-4

Find a comfortable place to sit, and relax for a few minutes. Let any extraneous thoughts or worries leave your mind as you prepare to listen to the music.

When you are relaxed, turn on some instrumental music. Try the classical music stations on your radio. As you listen to the music, pay close attention to the different sounds. Does the music remind you of anything? A person? A place? Open yourself to the sounds and let them guide your imagination. Let the music be the sound track to your inner visual experience.

The images that come to mind as you listen may or may not make sense to you. Let them come . . . and watch the products of your natural creative process emerge from inside you. By releasing your mind from the conventional drudgery of work and everyday existence, you can have access to more of your creative ideas and energy.

Once you have turned on the switch releasing your creativity with music, you can feel renewed creative energy in all areas of your life. You can continue to replenish and inspire your creative self by using the music that is available to you all the time, simply by listening.

Another means of using music's inspirational quality is by learning how to target specific types of music in order to increase the creative nature of your work. You have probably used music to cook, clean, or jog by in order to lessen the boredom of the task and put some excitement into it. In so doing, you were also inviting yourself to undertake these activities in a more creative manner. You can find out if, or how, music can increase the creative component of your work by experimenting. For example, what happens when you listen to energetic music in your office before you begin your day? Or, would listening to upbeat music around three o'clock in the afternoon help energize your creativity in order to do more than "make it through the next two hours"?

Many professionals use music as a powerful source of inspiration. A psychotherapist we know listens to music she finds soothing before seeing her clients. She finds that the music helps her feel more open to her creative resources when she works. In the intensive-care unit of one of New York City's major hospitals, the nurses keep the radio tuned to a popular disco station constantly. The music keeps them going both physically and emotionally and helps them cope with the nature of the work. The steady, lively beat is creatively stimulating, and inspires them to feel alive in a setting so often associated with illness and sorrow.

There is a way that listening to music can be a creative force in your daily life. Take the time to explore your individual creative responses to different types of music so that you can make this powerful resource work for you.

• Making Music for Creativity Development

Many of us feel silly, embarrassed, or scared at the thought of singing. We are convinced that we can't sing, because of what we were told in school or by our families. When we are brave enough to try, chances are that our tones don't sound as pleasant as we would like. This can be discouraging and is the reason why so many of us give up and miss out on the use of this natural spring of creativity in our lives. Everyone is born with a voice and has the right to sing out loud!

Singing *is* a creative act. It is a means of expressing who we are. We create sound where once there was silence. Each tone we emit is a unique sound; each song is the singer's own interpretation of the melody and rhythm; each melody that we hum during the day is evidence of our creative human nature. Did you ever realize that you have had a source of artistic, creative ability within you at all times? Your voice, your private creative instrument, can produce a wide variety of sounds. By making friends with your voice, you can acquaint yourself with who you are in a new way and connect with a joyful, creative means of expression. Earlier you learned why and how singing along with familiar music can help stimulate and satisfy your creative needs. Here we will explore more ways to use singing and playing an instrument to help develop specific creative skills.

Out of the natural desire to create sound as a young child, you probably made musical instruments out of a score of household items, such as pots and pans, candy wrappers, combs, and rubber bands. The need for creativity and sound-making is still a part of you today. However, attractive musical instruments are not as accessible as the sound-makers we used as children, and many people dismiss their desire to play an instrument, due to lack of time, money, talent, or initiative. In so doing, they lose access to a significant avenue of creative growth.

You may already have been aware that learning music can help you become more creative in the arts. Did you know, however, that singing and playing an instrument can help you become more creative in other areas as well?

"Direct music participation appears to have a significant positive effect on the development of characteristics of creativity."[5] Research in the fields of music education and creativity reveals that general creative potential can be stimulated by the active pursuit of music. In one study conducted with high school students, it was found that music-making increased the participants' word fluency and their ability to elaborate on their ideas and thoughts.[6] These are two ways in which we use our creative abilities throughout the day, either in conversation or in written work.

The study of a musical instrument, including the voice, calls for our learning new creative skills and exploring new creative options, which in turn contribute to greater general creativity. Practicing musical skills is a particularly effective means of contributing to total creative growth, because of the natural role of music-making in our developmental history. Music has always been a familiar means by which we express ourselves. It can continue to foster creative thought and action in your adult life now if only you make room in your day for its gifts.

If you have ever played an instrument, you probably know that once you have learned the notes of a particular passage, any number of creative options await you. Will you play it loud or soft, or alternate between the two? How fast or slowly will you play it? Will you accent any of the notes for emphasis, or play them all the same? Will you adopt a smooth, flowing style or a short, crisp one? Each option represents another possibility for self-expression. You can experiment with them all as you explore which feels right for you at the moment.

Here's a musical creativity builder that everyone can do each day:

Exercise 6-5

The next time you find yourself singing or humming a song, choose one phrase (the last line of "Happy Birthday," for example) and try singing it five different ways. Below are some possibilities:

- Start loud and get softer (and vice versa).
- Sing it as slowly as you can, then as quickly.
- Make pauses for dramatic effect.
- Sing it with a foreign accent.
- Pretend you're singing to someone you love.
- Pretend you're singing to someone you dislike.
- Pretend you're Luciano Pavarotti.
- Pretend you're Dolly Parton.
- Sing it shyly.
- Sing out with confidence.

If this seems silly to you, it's probably because of the childlike aspect of this exercise. But this child*like,* not child*ish,* nature in all of us can enhance, not detract from, our adulthood. This is the part of us that creates at will and remembers how to play. Try this exercise when you're in a private place (the shower seems to be the most popular setting) and out of earshot. You may be overjoyed to rediscover the sheer fun involved in playing with sound.

Making use of the options available to you in a given situation by playing an instrument or singing is, as we've said, a method of developing your general creativity. In addition, the mere knowledge that you have added the new creative dimension of music-making in your life can have an impact on your creative frame of mind. The confidence that results from playing music remains with you, and can directly influence the way you approach tasks that await you at home and at work. Without even realizing it, you may think, act, and respond more creatively as a result of your musical endeavors. The inspiration that comes from practicing an instrument in the morning can be carried over to your day's work. Even singing creatively in the shower can give you the confidence necessary to be more imaginative on the job.

There is another way that music-making can affect your general creative expression. If you have ever felt blocked or stuck when trying to complete a task, substituting one mode of expression for another, such as using music instead of language, can result in a renewed flow of creative energy, not just in the music, but when you return to working with language as well.[7] How does this happen? First of all, the pressure of working on the original material is relieved, which can relax you. Also, you're taking a break in order to reconnect with yourself. Most importantly, however, you will have been playing music and experiencing the inherent creativity that flows in each melody you play and song that you sing.

The next time you feel that your creativity is being inhibited in one area, try going for a walk and singing or whistling to yourself, or sitting down and playing your instrument, or putting on a record and humming along. These activities can stimulate, recharge, and renew the creativity needed to complete your work.

In addition to the ways mentioned above, the creativity inherent in music-making can have a crucial impact on physical, as well as mental, health. Music therapists working with terminally ill patients have seen that very often such patients experience relief of pain while making music, and, as a direct result, a resurgence of strength to fight their disease. The ability to produce music is life-affirming and instills courage and hope.

One of the most moving accounts of the impact of creative music-making on physical health is that written by Norman Cousins, who, with the help of an excellent physician and by creative, untraditional means, changed the course of an illness that threatened his life. In his book *Anatomy of an Illness,* which tells of his recovery, he describes a visit with Pablo Casals. Casals, although renowned for his virtuosity on the cello, was also proficient on the piano. When Cousins visited him, the writer witnessed a profound example of the ability of music to help heal the body and to create new resources for life. Cousins begins with a description of Casals as he was when Cousins first met him, then tells of the cellist's incredible transformation, with the help of his music:

I met him for the first time at his home in Puerto Rico just before his ninetieth birthday. I was fascinated by his daily routine. About 8 A.M. his lovely young wife, Marta, would help him to start his day. His various infirmities made it difficult for him to dress himself. Judging from his difficulty in walking and from the way he held his arms, I guessed he was suffering from rheumatoid arthritis. His emphysema was evident in his labored breathing. He came into the living room on Marta's arm. He was badly stooped. His head was pitched forward and he walked with a shuffle. His hands were swollen and his fingers were clenched.

Even before going to the breakfast table, Don Pablo went to the piano—which, I learned, was a daily ritual. He arranged himself with some difficulty on the piano bench, then with some discernible effort raised his swollen and clenched fingers above the keyboard.

I was not prepared for the miracle that was about to happen. The fingers slowly unlocked and reached towards the keys like the buds of a plant towards the sunlight. His back straightened. He seemed to breathe more freely. Now his fingers settled on the keys. . . . He hummed as he played, then said that Bach spoke to him here—and placed his hands over his heart.

Then he plunged into a Brahms concerto and his fingers, now agile and powerful, raced across the keyboard with dazzling speed. His entire body seemed fused with the music; it was no longer stiff and shrunken, but supple and graceful and completely free of arthritic coils.

Having finished the piece, he stood up by himself, far straighter and taller than when he had come into the room. He walked to the breakfast table with no trace of a shuffle, ate heartily, talked animatedly, finished the meal, then went for a walk on the beach.[8]

Later that day, Casals went to the cello:

He began to play. His fingers, hand and arms were in sublime coordination as they responded to the demands of his brain for the controlled beauty of movement and tone.

Twice in one day I had seen the miracle. A man almost ninety, beset with the infirmities of old age, was able to cast off his afflictions, at least temporarily, because he knew he had something of overriding importance to do. There was no mystery about the way it worked, for it happened every day. Creativity for Pablo Casals was the source of his own cortisone. It is doubtful whether any anti-inflammatory medication he would have taken would have been as powerful or as safe as the substances produced by the interaction of his mind and body.[9]

Creative music experiences can bring you new opportunities for growth whether your health is failing or just returning, and provide the healing energy needed for a meaningful life.

• Improvisation for Creativity Development

Music improvisation is the art of creating music spontaneously in the moment. There are many ways to improvise. One way is by making up a song on the spot. Another is by sitting down at a piano (or with any other instrument) and letting your fingers wander over the keys, listening to what emerges. A third kind takes more practice: Jazz musicians engage in this type of improvisation, which involves the free interpretation of melody, harmony, and rhythm within a predetermined musical structure.

The thought of improvising is scary to most people. When making up a song or freely improvising on an instrument, there's no musical structure established, so it's hard to know how to begin or how to continue. Also, we may dislike some of the music, which can be discouraging. Jazz improvisation requires skills that many of us haven't developed and that may appear beyond our reach.

When improvising, most people experience a significantly greater sense of their own creativity than with other forms of music-making. Improvisation is the epitome of the creative process, and is an ability that we are all born with. *Everyone* can learn how to improvise, and experience his or her creative powers in this way.

The singing exercise you did earlier (see page 61) is an example of improvisation. Since the melody and words are familiar, there is a musical structure from which to improvise. The structure provides some musical security.

Here's another exercise in improvisation, which uses a different type of structure:

Exercise 6-6

The next time you can spend a few minutes at a piano, sit down and locate five adjacent white notes. Any five notes will do, as long as they are in a line. Find other five-note groupings and choose one that is pleasing to you.

Using only these five notes, play them one at a time, first in a row, and then out of order, to create new melodic lines. Experiment with different rhythms. Try playing both loud and soft.

You may not have believed that you could create melodies and rhythms, but in doing this exercise, you are doing just that! By improvising, you create sound—in the moment, out of silence. You may be quite surprised at the pleasant sounds you are making.

Now choose a different set of white notes, or a set of *eight* adjacent white notes, and repeat the exercise. You'll have a different but equally creative experience.

By adding a black note or two, you can create some dissonance. It may sound jazzy or it may sound unpleasant. See what happens as you continue playing freely. Let yourself wander into new musical territory by adding one or two new notes at a time; then return to your original set of notes.

If you already play an instrument, try improvising freely within a scale. Take all the notes of a D-major scale, for example, and create some melodies. Compose a joyful melody, a melancholy melody, an exotic melody (you may want to add a few extra notes for this one!), and a boring melody. By moving your fingers in any direction, a melody is created. It may not be familiar, and some of your creations may be less satisfying than others, but they are melodies nonetheless and they are yours.

Exercise 6-7

Here's another improvisation exercise, which is particularly easy and enjoyable.

Again at the piano, this time you will be playing only the black notes. Each group of five notes comprises what is called the pentatonic, or five-note, scale. Play the black notes in a row, starting from the middle of the piano and moving your fingers to the right, to acquaint yourself with the sound.

If your first impression is that it sounds Oriental, you are not alone. Much Oriental music has been built on this scale. The way in which the notes of the pentatonic scale are spaced lend it an open sound relatively free of dissonance, which is why many people find it so attractive.

To play a pentatonic improvisation, strike the black notes in a row, then out of order, with your right hand while holding down one black note from the bass of the piano with your left. As you play, create different rhythms with your right hand. Continue to hold down your bass note underneath the melody for as long as the tone lasts, then play it again.

For a dramatic change, continue to play as you have been with your right hand, but change your bass note. Make sure you remain only on the black notes. Changing the bass note makes such a big difference because the depth of the tone implies a harmony. We hear, or feel, more of a harmonic presence even though we are playing just one note. Change the bass note whenever you wish, and enjoy the variety of your music-making.

Also, try this exercise while pressing down on the sustaining pedal—the foot pedal on the right. This will blend the sound, creating a dreamlike effect.

Your ability to create music in this way proves an important point: Every human being is a musician by nature, and improvisation is the celebration of this inborn trait. The more you experience your ability to improvise, the more you can transfer this skill to other areas of your life. Improvisation is the exact opposite of rigidity; it means taking chances and trusting your efforts, no matter the outcome. Creative cooks improvise constantly, adding an extra ingredient here and there to add interest, novelty, and flavor to a familiar recipe. Sometimes the results are not exactly as desired, but more often a surprisingly delicious dish is the reward.

Improvisation is also a tremendous help in social situations that go awry. When you plan a picnic or outdoor event and are greeted with inclement weather, your skill in creative improvisation can help you find a satisfying alternative to canceling and missing out on an enjoyable afternoon with friends.

There are always ups and downs in improvisation. When improvising music, you may love the sounds you make at times and dislike them at others. The emotional high one can get from a creative musical experience is often tremendous, however, so the benefits far outweigh the risks.

Thinking and acting creatively is a way to shine as a unique individual. Invite more music into your life! You can revive the creative spirit you had as a child and let it work for you now, as an adult.

7

Discover Joy
Through Music

Music is a source of indescribable joy. One of the most powerful aspects of our work together as music therapists is the ease with which we can provide our clients with pleasurable musical experiences. The effect of these experiences on their depression, anxieties, and listlessness, among other symptoms, is pronounced. When they are involved in musical experiences, their healthy impulses tend to emerge.[1]

It is an unfortunate trait of our society that the expression and sharing of joy are often discouraged. In order to share joyous feelings, we may feel we need an excuse, such as a holiday, a promotion, or a special occasion. We may often rely upon alcohol or drugs, thinking that such artificial stimulants will help us feel and express this natural, and exhilarating, human emotion.

At one time in our lives, however, feeling and expressing joy was second nature. During our childhood, each new discovery about life brought a flood of joyous feeling and excitement. Every time we were stimulated by the simplest sound, movement, or color, we audibly revealed our delight.

These wondrous feelings encouraged us to continue discovering and growing. Through feeling and expressing our joys, we continue to learn what is healthy for us, what is enriching to us, and what we naturally crave in our lives.

When we express our joys as children, we experience reactions from those around us. As transactional analyst Claude Steiner writes: "Children love to run and jump, skip, tumble, scream, cry, laugh and express themselves emotionally. Emotional expression is pleasurable, but is often ill received by parents, who are annoyed by its energy or honesty. When parents unilaterally squelch and curtail the emotional expressions and, consequently, the pleasures of children, they are laying down the injunctions and attributions of joylessness."[2] If, in childhood, your feelings and expressions were celebrated, chances are that you feel comfortable about expressing your emotions now as an adult. If, however, your elation at discovering the world proved too noisy for your household or gave your mother a headache, you probably internalized negative messages about expressing joy, and withheld your feelings to relieve the pressure of the situation.

In a child's mind, the observation "I'd better not share my joy because it makes Mom mad" can become the decision "I won't share my joy." This decision can remain operative until something or someone challenges us to change it. For example, later on in life, by meeting someone who feels fine about sharing joy, we can realize that the environment around us has changed, and get "permission" from the new person and environment to express our feelings. By inviting into your life people who have made positive decisions about feeling and sharing their joy, you can begin to change your own, negative decisions about expressing positive feelings.

Many of us have made decisions that allow for the sharing of joy only under certain circumstances. For example, "I will share my joy only when everyone else is joyous" or "I need a good reason to express my joy" are decisions that contribute to the often cheerless condition of our society. They represent an internal recognition of the desire and need to express joy in our lives, but allow for it only in a limited manner.

Many work environments further reinforce these decisions by discouraging the expression of joy except at the "office holiday party" or other organized celebrations. There is hardly room to recognize our true joyous feelings when we are told when and how to feel them by parents, bosses, advertisers, and social rules. Our joys are discouraged much of the time for fear they will get in the way of our productivity (when the opposite is more likely to be true!), and encouraged at certain fixed times that do not necessarily conform to the natural flow of feeling with which we are born. Around holiday times, for example, we even begin to feel that we *should* feel joyous, "get the holiday spirit," and that something is wrong with us if we don't. That is why depression is so prevalent at holiday times. After withholding our natural joyous expressions all year, when society's designated time for showing joy rolls around and we don't feel like it, we may fear that something is wrong with us.

In certain cases, we make decisions to suppress not only the expression of joy but also the experiencing of the feeling itself. "I won't feel joy" or "I won't feel happy" are decisions that may stem from a family situation in which the children receive more attention and love when they are sad, angry, or scared than when they are feeling good. These children can recognize that in order to get their basic needs met they must only feel and express emotions that support their parents' joyless existence. As adults, these persons may use such expressions as "Misery loves company" to reinforce their beliefs.

You can change the decisions you once made about feeling and expressing joy by letting yourself get in touch with your natural reactions to the people, places, and things around you so as to rediscover what truly brings you pleasure. We will show you how to do this with music, a source of joyous feeling and expression since the beginning of time. Consider the following suggestions:

1. *Attend concerts.* Watch how the musicians express themselves, and how members of the audience receive the sounds. In this permissive environment, you can let yourself take in the music that's being played for you. Let your natural joyous response to sound emerge as you applaud the artists or, on your way home, sing the songs you heard.

2. *Listen to street musicians.* Take the time to look around you and observe the facial and bodily reactions of the gathered crowd. If the music is upbeat, you will probably see a lot of tapping feet. Music is irresistible! Try to ignore familiar critical messages you may be hearing in your head, such as "Showing feelings in public is silly and embarrassing" or "I can't enjoy this music the way others do." Let yourself take part in the joy that others share through musical exchange.

3. *Listen to the radio.* The radio is another source of music and thus another source of joy. What's more, radio announcers, disc jockeys, and program participants are quick to share their excitement about particular songs and their feelings about the music they play. As you hear their comments, acknowledge

their enthusiasm for the music they like. Then listen to your own internal comments. . . . Do you feel similarly about the pieces they mentioned? What feelings were elicited in you by the music they played? Be aware of the enthusiasm that music generates in the general public, and learn about your own natural enthusiasm for the music you hear.

• Listening to Music for Joy

Listening to music is usually regarded as a passive experience. But even when we are not consciously aware of it, we physically, intellectually, and emotionally respond to the sound vibrations around us. In order to reconnect with that underlying feeling of joy and other emotions, you must become an *active* listener. Active listening means listening to music as an activity in itself, rather than using it as a background. In this way, you welcome your unconscious reactions to sound, which can stimulate feelings, thoughts, and behavior, as well as develop an awareness of your natural joyous reactions to music.

A world of expressive possibilities and emotional experiences awaits you in the wealth of music that has been recorded for listening. The great works of classical music have not just existed through time; they have thrived. Why has this music remained as a stable component of so many cultures? The great composers of our past were able to manipulate the elements of music (rhythm, melody, harmony, form, dynamics, timbre, and texture) in such a way as to provide emotional stimulation for generations of listeners. The flow of the music taps into the flow of human feeling, and the crescendos and decrescendos of the sound correspond to the rise and fall of our emotional states. We can also learn about and experience emotions that we were unaware were within us. Aaron Copland, noted American composer and teacher, feels that "a masterwork awakens in us reactions of a spiritual order that are already in us, or waiting to be aroused."[3] The joy of discovering our full emotional capacities can be brought about through listening to music.

It is not just classical music, however, that is so potentially enriching. *Any* type of music can evoke powerful feelings in you, depending on your tastes, your mood, the environment, the time of day, and who you're with. The particular blend of harmonies, rhythms, and melodies in a piece of music may affect you one day and not the next. Then again, there may be certain pieces or types of music that will always evoke a strong reaction of joy in you. The important thing is to actively listen:

Exercise 7-1

When you listen to a piece of music, *really* listen—with your whole body. Try closing your eyes, so that your auditory sense is heightened. Let the sounds wash over you, and be aware of your physical responses to what you hear. Pay attention to your breathing and your heartbeat. Do they quicken or relax? Does the music "feel" good to you?

Since this listening exercise is geared toward experiencing positive feelings, if the music is too dissonant, rhythmic, or atonal for your taste, begin again with another piece. Find the kind of music that attracts you and feels right for you in the moment. Listen to the contour of the melody line. Follow it as it rises, peaks, and descends. Feel the pulse of the rhythm. Let the sounds seep in through your skin as you become one with the music.

Remember that there is nothing wrong with acknowledging your feelings and expressing them as you hear the music. Responding to music with emotion is natural, and the goal of this exercise is for you to restore this natural process in order to let more joy into your life. So, if you feel tears coming on as you listen, let them come! And let your body rock or move whatever way it wants to.

Listen to this music a few times. As you become familiar with the piece, you open up yet another avenue for joy. You will begin to hear more in the music and, as a result, *feel* more. You may again be tempted to sing the melody or move with the rhythm. This is our natural response to the creative stimulation of the sound.

Here are some more ways to bring joy into your life by becoming an active music listener:

1. *Allow more time in your life for listening to music.*
2. *Experience yourself as a listener to the music of different eras, different cultures, different composers, and different performers.* One friend of ours once chose a composer a month and spent

a few hours weekly becoming familiar with that composer's music and his own reactions to it. In so doing, he learned a lot about music in general, while providing himself with new emotional experiences.

3. *Try listening to a different radio station each week, or exchanging records and tapes with friends.* As you expand your listening repertoire, take note of the songs or pieces that communicate joyous messages to you. Let these messages teach you that it's O.K. to feel, express, and share your joys. Let the music give you permission to feel.

4. *In addition to listening alone, try listening with a friend or with your family.* The sharing of joy through music can greatly enhance your experience.

5. *Listen to both recorded and live music.* We respond to each differently. Note how you experience the one as compared with the other, and which triggers more joyous responses in you.

As you become an active listener and learn which music most brings out your joy, you can use this music whenever you like to elicit such a response in yourself. Considering that our moods and feelings change from one moment to the next, a favorite song may not always evoke feelings of joy. Chances are, though, that once you associate a song with strong positive emotions, these emotions will *usually* surface whenever you hear it.

A favorite song can get you into the mood for a social event, help you through the last mile of a long race, make standing in traffic tolerable, inspire you to try something new, or just make you feel good all over.

One of our friends almost always responds joyfully to certain rock-and-roll "oldies." The rhythm makes her want to move, and the music carries with it associations to wonderful times spent with friends. When rock and roll is too fast-paced for her mood, certain classical works bring on a pleasurable feeling. One New York City physician told us that he gets emotionally turned on by jazz. He feels lighthearted when hearing Duke Ellington's music, and relishes spending evenings listening and keeping time to the music. As you become an active listener, let yourself explore your reactions to the music you hear, and become acquainted with the sounds that feel joyous to you.

• Making Music for Joy

There is a youthful, joyful sound-maker in all of us. In Chapter 1, we described the crucial function that sound-making serves for us as infants and young children. By making sounds, we satisfy our needs for attention, stimulation, tension release, entertainment, communication with self and others, and self-expression. These needs still exist in us as adults, yet we tend to dismiss the desire to satisfy them as "childish." As adults, we take on the responsibilities of home and work so seriously at times that our personal needs become secondary. As a result, we can feel unmotivated, neglected, and stressed. We can have problems communicating with others and, at the same time, become increasingly out of touch with ourselves. We can become more and more unfulfilled. The decisions we may have made as youngsters, not to feel or share our joys, can become rules we live by as adults. We need ways to recapture the joys of expression that came so naturally to us as children—ways that feel comfortable to us as adults.

Music-making is one satisfying and fun remedy for this condition. By making sounds, you awaken your capacity to express and experience the joy of childhood in an adult fashion. Playing an instrument and singing are two accessible means of satisfying these basic human needs, reversing the negative decisions you made about expressing yourself as a child, and inviting more joy into your life.

There are as many ways to make music as there are people who wish to try. There are different instruments and different types of music. There are pieces of music available for people of all ages, tastes, musical experience, and backgrounds.

Aside from this, there is you. There is your own special way of handling an instrument and of making sounds. If you have had no musical training or have had negative or painful experiences with unsupportive teachers, you may be thinking "*I* can't play an instrument!" or "If these authors knew me, they would never write this." Well, you may indeed have no musical talent; you may sing out of tune or you may have been told not to play or sing. You *still* can reap the joys of playing an instrument or singing if you want to. Not only is it *possible* for you to be involved in music-making, it is your *right* to do so. By virtue of the fact that you were born with a voice, you can be assured that music is a part of you.

If you play an instrument or sing, you can express yourself in a form of beauty every day. When you take the time, however little, to practice and play the music you love, you become a part of the creative pulse that stimulates life and excitement. When you join your voice with those of others during a concert or in front of a campfire, you become one with your environment and share in the harmony of life. You stretch and expand your world, releasing the confining tensions of daily living, and open your heart to the joyous healing energies of music.

Here are some ways to bring more joy into your life through singing and/or playing an instrument:

1. *Play and sing the music you love.* Don't play pieces just because your teacher likes them; make sure that you have a positive connection to the music you learn.

2. *Learn to sight-read.* You can then experience the instant gratification that comes from exploring new music and playing it well.

3. *Play for others.* The word *performance* usually terrifies most people, because of the perfection usually demanded in common performing situations. Design your own performance criteria instead! We suggest that only caring, interested people be invited (you may want to start with an audience of one supportive friend at first), that mistakes be allowed—even expected—in the playing of the pieces, and that the goal be simply to enjoy making music for yourself and your listeners. Your joy, when communicated through the music, makes much more of an impact on the listener than a few wrong notes. Consider how terrific it would feel to be proud of your music-making and to share it with others.

4. *Join an ensemble.* Feel the tremendous high that comes from sharing in the music experience with others. Being part of a musical group can become addictive. Many people who participated in choruses, orchestras, or bands in high school or college

can describe in detail the memorable experiences they had—
and miss years later.

There's no reason why wonderful music experiences should exist
only in the past. In every city there are amateur groups that welcome community members. You can find the right music-making
situation for your tastes, needs, abilities, and life-style.

• Peak Experiences with Music

Just as a vicious cycle is created when we don't meet our needs,
a healthy cycle is created when we do. When you make music,
you can experience the greatest of joys. These joyous musical
experiences stay with you always, reminding you of what you
are capable of feeling about yourself and your world.

Music has always been associated with joyous feelings. However,
as there are many types of music, there are also varying levels
of joy. Sometimes when listening to music, we are filled with a
quiet warmth that some would describe as joy; at other times,
dancing wildly to an upbeat hit would be described as joyous.
Music can trigger an extremely high level of feeling, however,
that goes beyond the usual pleasurable emotions with which many
of us are familiar. This is called "peak experience."

Abraham Maslow (see Chapter 6) discovered valuable information about peak experiences after studying them for many years.
A peak experience is a moment of transcendence, an indescribable
rush, in which we feel in harmony with the world and feel that
life is just the way it's meant to be. In these moments, we feel
flooded with joyous, blissful emotions. Peak experiences have been
reported occurring through involvement with all of the arts, as
well as with many other activities. They are reported to occur
most frequently, however, in association with music, and with sex.
*It is classical music and rhythmic music with dancing that most
often trigger the peak experience.* [4] The people who were having
such experiences were not trained musicians or dancers; they were
from all walks of life, responding joyfully to the powerful medium
of music.

These peak experiences, or moments of bliss and transcendence,
have major consequences. They can lead both to the release of
anxiety and to the development of sensory awareness and sponta-

neity. Most important, however, is the strengthened sense of identity that comes from the peak experience, for this can help you feel more positive about your life.[5]

Close your eyes and think for a minute. Have you ever had a moment of ecstacy during which you felt a unity with the world around you and regarded the world as perfect and right? If you have, do you now tremble with emotion as you remember the moment? If your answer is yes, you have probably had what we are describing here as a peak experience.

Was music part of your experience? Think back to a rally in which you may have participated, where your voice was heard among many . . . to a special concert . . . to singing Christmas carols among family and friends, by a fire or under a starlit sky. Or was music the background to an intimate expression of love with someone special?

Many people who have had peak experiences are reluctant to acknowledge them for fear of rejection or isolation. Also, sometimes these powerful feelings are unfamiliar and therefore hard to express. If you have had one or many peak experiences, let yourself remember those moments now. They are gifts to be cherished. If you have never experienced this phenomenon, by opening yourself to music you open yourself to the possibility of enjoying peak experiences as well.

Music has survived throughout time because of its ability to bring joy to our lives. It accompanies profound religious moments—and our most intimate expressions with others. It is almost always present as we celebrate the joyous landmark occasions in our lives. Imagine a wedding without music!

Music brings joy in its wake. Joy is a basic human need, and the peak experiences that can be brought about through musical involvement serve a vital function in our lives. According to Maslow, they contribute to self-actualization, which is the realization of our full potential.

In other words, it is *necessary* to feel joy in order to live your life to the fullest. Although experiencing all of our feelings is fundamental to being emotionally fit, being able to feel *joyous* is an especially crucial building block to our total health. If you have spent your life hiding your feelings, limiting your capacity for feeling joy, and never discovering peak experiences, you have been putting yourself under undue strain. Let music teach you what you've been missing! By actively listening to and playing music, you can begin to challenge your negative outlook on self-expression, and joyously contribute to your continued growth as a person.

8
Music for Greater Self-Esteem

Self-esteem is the powerful by-product of an awareness of, acceptance of, love for, and appreciation of who you are as a human being. Self-esteem is essential for healthy living and for successful intimate relationships with others. If you are always holding others in greater esteem than yourself, you will probably do more to meet their needs than your own. This results in your needs being frustrated, and the continuation of unequal communication in your interpersonal relationships.

The development of self-awareness is crucial to greater self-esteem, and one way to increase self-awareness is to listen to yourself—to the voices deep inside that tell you what your needs are. Maslow calls these the "impulse voices," or "inner signals." By doing so, you get in touch with what you truly like or dislike, never mind what others think. You recover the ability to determine when you need to sleep, eat, or drink, regardless of the accepted schedules to which you usually adapt.[1] Gaining self-esteem involves the contacting of these true likes and dislikes, needs and wants, and the acceptance of the feelings, thoughts, and actions that emerge as a result. This can be achieved by listening to, singing, and playing music.

• Listening to Music for Self-Esteem

Listening to music is an easy, accessible means of re-establishing contact with your true inner self. Your musical tastes are a part of your identity as a person. As an infant, you were instinctively aware of which sounds in your environment were nurturing and healthy for you and which felt unsafe. The sounds of the environment were stimulants for your physical and vocal responses, and contributed to the development of your identity. Music can serve the same function in your life now, as an adult. When you listen to music that feels good to you, you create an environment conducive to positive attitudes toward the self and others. This is the healthy balance necessary for the increase of self-esteem.

Take a few minutes to listen to a piece of music you love— *without* doing chores or anything else. Find a comfortable place to sit or lie down, and actively listen to the music. Pretend that you are the audience at a private concert and that the music is being played only for you.

Can you say what it is about this piece of music that you love so much? Is it the rhythm? The tune? The harmony? Or do you simply love it and love the way it makes you feel? There's no need to know *why* you love the music, but there is a need for you to know *that* you love it. Be aware of your feelings about the music, and know that each time you listen to and feel the sounds, you listen to and feel your individuality, strength, and positive sense of self.

Unfortunately, through the media, critics, and peer pressure, our true reactions to music are often squelched. Subconsciously, we may be attracted to a new hit song before even *hearing* it because of what we've been told about it. We are constantly being drawn away from our natural reactions to a particular piece of music, usually for commercial purposes. It is those reactions, however, that can provide us with information about ourselves, help us to know who we are and to define our identities as individuals.

Your reactions to the different elements of even a single piece of music can teach you much about your own internal rhythms and pace, the flexibility of your rhythms from moment to moment, your emotional connections to the rise and fall of melody, your individual experience of harmonies as they affect your mood, and your ability to flow with the shifting intensity of the dynamics of the music. In this next exercise, we will show you how to use music listening in this new way:

Exercise 8-1

To begin, choose music that is relatively new to you, either by turning to an unfamiliar radio station or by putting on a record

you haven't heard in a while. As you listen, keep the following
questions in mind:

1. Do you like this music? What do you like or dislike about it?
2. Does this music match your rhythmic pace at this moment,
   or is it too fast or too slow?
3. What do you feel about the melody? Does its rise and fall
   have an effect on you?
4. Is the music too consonant or too dissonant for your tastes?
   What do you feel about the harmony?
5. Does the music bring up any memories for you? If so, what
   is it like to experience these memories now?
6. How do you feel as the music gets louder and softer and varies
   in dynamic intensity?
7. How does the music as a whole make you feel?

Listening in this way can teach you about your inner self. Your
reactions to the rhythm of a piece of music reveal your internal
rhythmic clock, your pace as you move through your day. If you
felt that the music you listened to was too fast or too slow for
your comfort, this is because the natural desire to have your
rhythms matched was frustrated. As mentioned in Chapter 2, one
of the basic security and self-esteem needs of the infant is to
have his physical and emotional rhythms matched by those around
him. This need carries into adulthood, which explains why we
search out and prefer people with whom we can be "in sync."

Think about your closest friends and loved ones. Are their
rhythms similar to your own? Do you enjoy the challenge of the
syncopation that occurs as your different rhythms mix, or are you
bothered by the problems that a difference in pace creates? How
do you handle yourself when you are faced with rhythms different
from your own? Do you wind up feeling good about yourself in
these situations, or bad? Are you the one to always adapt your
rhythms to those of the other, or do you always demand that
his match yours? Or have you found a way to get in rhythmic
harmony so that both you and your partner feel good about yourselves as the conflict resolves?

Here's an example from everyday life. Think of the frustration
you may feel as you wait for a slow bank teller to complete your

transaction when you are late for work. You may choose to take care of your frustration over the teller's slower rhythms by becoming more assertive and asking him to hurry. This would be an attempt to motivate him to pick up the tempo of his work so as to meet your needs. Or you may take a deep breath, tell yourself to relax, and wait it out. This would be an attempt to get in sync by adapting your rhythms to the environment. In both cases, your need to do something to find a common tempo is instinctive.

By being aware of your inner rhythms and your feelings as they meet the outer rhythms of the environment, you can learn how to get your needs met in a harmonious way. Each time you unnecessarily adapt your rhythms to the environment, your sense of self-esteem can diminish. When your rhythms are acknowledged, your importance is recognized and your sense of self-esteem is raised another notch. Active music listening can help you build awareness of your rhythmic needs so that you can create situations in which they are satisfied.

Let's come back to listening exercise 8-1 (pages 79–80). As you listened to the music, what did you feel about the melody? How did you react to the contour (rise and fall) of the melody line? Did it bring out the singer in you? The romantic in you? Many people feel the intensity of the music rise as the melody rises, and experience more intense feelings at this point. This is reflective of what happens to our voices as we speak with greater intensity. A rush of emotions tends to make our voices go higher, as well as louder.

If you are comfortable with your own and another person's expressions of different feeling levels, you will probably fully enjoy the ranges of emotional intensity that melodic tension creates. If, however, you feel threatened by or uncomfortable with the vocal expression of intense emotion, you may have a negative reaction when you hear this happening in the music. Let yourself know what feels comfortable and uncomfortable to you about the melody you listened to. What emotions did it stimulate? Accept these reactions as a part of yourself, and know that by bringing your feelings into awareness you are in a position to know more about who you are. This knowledge will aid in the development of your self-esteem. If you are unhappy about your reactions to the music, realize that you can change what feels uncomfortable to you only by being aware of what it is.

Melodies and memories tend to go hand in hand. Did you have any memories or associations with the melody you heard? Did they feel good to you or uncomfortable? If "uncomfortable," do you have a good idea why?

How did you react to the harmonies of the piece you listened to? Were they dissonant or consonant? Did they match your mood at the moment, or were they disturbing? Did your mood change as a result of hearing the music?

Our response to harmony in music is a metaphor for our reactions to harmony in our lives. How do you feel about dissonances when they occur between you and others? If you have learned that it is O.K. to experience dissonance, that you can work with it and flow into consonance as a result, you may be comfortable hearing dissonant music as well. An example of this would be feeling that it's all right to engage in a verbal argument with someone, because you know it will help clarify rather than harm or threaten your relationship. If, however, conflicts and interpersonal dissonances are especially frightening or uncomfortable, you will probably have a strong negative reaction to dissonant sounds. What images are revealed as you listen to dissonance? Are these connected to memories you have of strained times in your life?

If you had tried this exercise among a group of people, you would have found each person's reactions to the harmonic quality of the music to be different. Your reactions were the combined elements of your mood and feelings at the moment, your emotional and cultural experiences with consonance and dissonance, your musical likes and dislikes, and your individual nature. By accepting and honoring your personal reactions to the music you hear, you can get more in touch with yourself, develop greater self-awareness, and consequently feel a stronger sense of self-esteem.

Now think about the dynamics, or the "louds and softs," of the piece you heard. How did you react to the dynamic flow? Just as the rise and fall in pitch of the melody can indicate the highs and lows of emotional intensity, the crescendos and decrescendos are symbolic of the changing volumes of emotional expression. Did your feelings build as the music got louder and subside as it got softer? Or did you experience the opposite? Did the quiet, tender passages evoke in you a more intense response than the louder episodes? It is also possible that you were untouched by the music. If so, was it a matter of musical taste—of not liking the music—or were you resisting the memories and feelings that might have surfaced had you let them?

Resistance to feeling the music is neither bad nor good. When we resist, we do so for a reason. Resistance is the protection we develop when we're not ready to know or face certain feelings or thoughts. Respect for our resistances maintains our self-esteem. When you feel resistant to hearing certain music, accept that there is a reason for it and that by being aware of it you can begin to understand it and eventually let it go. In this way you can become more open to the full richness of the listening experience.

There are other elements of the music, such as its form, texture, and timbre, to which you will respond as you learn to listen in this way. Sometimes it is the combination of all the elements of the piece that will affect you. The exquisite tapestry of rhythm, melody, harmony, dynamics, form, texture, and timbre can stir you deeply and unearth new awarenesses of yourself. Be conscious of the difference between how you felt before you did this exercise and how you feel now. Are you aware of a difference that you can attribute to the music? If so, can you articulate what this difference is?

In our awareness of our responses to music is the awareness of self. Your likes and dislikes, your tastes in sound, the feelings that emerged as you listened to the music, the associations and memories triggered by the music—all are a part of your unique personal identity. Most people react to this exercise with surprise, never having realized what music can reveal about the self. This discovery is the point of the exercise. When you listen to music in this way, it becomes a powerful source of self-knowledge, of which most people are unaware. Listening to music can become a way of contacting the "impulse voices" to which Maslow refers, and in so doing, contributing to the growth of your self-esteem.

• Making Music for Self-Esteem

The development of self-esteem through sound-making is an integral part of human development. As children, we delight in sound-making and experience the self-affirmation, as well as the ecstasy, that can result from musical expression. Peter Ostwald, a psychiatrist who has written extensively about the role of music in our lives, writes:

> When (one) whistles, he hears his own sound directly, and this, like speaking, singing, humming, or any other form of sound-making, gives him knowledge that he exists. It is like looking into a mirror or touching one's body. Such self-evaluative activities prove to the individual that he is alive, intact, and awake. It is the most immediate and reliable way to reassure oneself.[2]

Music-making through singing or playing an instrument can continue to serve these functions for us as adults. If you have ever chosen to play an instrument as a grownup, you probably did so because playing music feels good to you in one way or another. Some people find release in the relaxation that comes from making music, while others love the stimulation of creativity that's inherent in musical expression. No matter what the exact reasons are, music-making in any form adds a new dimension to your life. The sense of accomplishment, confidence, purpose, and release that musical expression brings can result in a tremendous increase in your sense of self-esteem. As Ostwald claims: "We use sounds in an effort to fulfill several human needs. The first of these is the need to be aware of ourselves—to establish and maintain a self image."[3]

This is the reason why it feels so good to be able to say "I'm a singer," "I'm studying the flute," or "I'm an amateur pianist." Being able to make music is something to be proud of! By studying music you become a trained musician, no matter how old you are. Age need not be a deterrant to the learning of musical skills. In fact, the experience and wisdom that often accompany the aging process can contribute to the most fulfilling musical expressions. Age can be a gift when it comes to understanding the depths of music.

When we surveyed people in the New York City area, many persons said they have always wanted to play an instrument or sing but don't, for a variety of reasons. Underlying this long-time desire is the belief that being able to make music in a satisfying way will build self-esteem. What is your musical fantasy? If you have secretly wanted to study music, you can make that wish a reality. We'll show you exactly how to do this in Chapters 11 and 12.

If you already sing or play an instrument, you can *increase* the natural boost to your self-esteem that you may already feel. One way is by developing a new way of paying attention to your music. The next time you use your instrument, begin with one phrase of a familiar piece. Play or sing the phrase and listen closely to the sounds. It is *your* body making the sounds as you sing, the dexterity of your fingers producing the music as you play; your breath moving wind through your flute, the coordination of your body producing complex rhythms on your drums, and the strength of your arms coaxing sound from your cello. Be conscious of this physical feeling of contacting and creating with your instrument.

While music brings more enrichment into your life, it is *you* who brings life to the music. Aside from being aware of the fact that you make the sounds, and of the physical sensations involved, listen now to *how* you make them. How do you sing the phrase? How do you choose to express those words in a way that's yours and yours alone? How do you bring meaning to those black lines and dots? The music is not only what is written on the page; the music is what you discover in between the notes. As you bring the music to life, and fill the silence around you with beautiful sound, so do you "enliven" your thoughts, feelings, and sense of self-esteem.

Repeat the phrase several times, and continue to listen to yourself and your music. Most of the time we listen only to the music and fail to connect the sounds with their source. Use your senses of vision and touch, as well as of hearing, to feel yourself as the music-maker.

By the time you have played or sung the phrase a few times, you will have mastered it, if you hadn't before you began. With mastery comes the deep sense of pride and pleasure of musical accomplishment.[4] The strong feelings of confidence and self-esteem that result make the necessary practice worthwhile.

By listening to the music that you love and that feels good to you, by listening in order to learn more about yourself and to develop self-awareness, by playing music or singing while listening to and feeling yourself as the creator of beautiful sound, and by developing mastery and musical accomplishment through repetition and practice, you can directly increase your sense of self-esteem. We invite you to make use of music, an endless resource of energy and joy, to continue to celebrate, discover, and proudly share who you are with yourself and with those around you.

9
Building
Confidence
with Music

Everyone wants to feel confident and strong. Feeling confident means knowing that you can meet the challenges of your life and handle them well. Confidence is energy—energy to succeed.

Each time we are confronted with a new situation, we must mobilize our energies in order to identify what needs to be done and how we are going to do it. Having a sense of confidence helps make this process easier. The ability to say "I can do it!" is essential for success on the job, at home, and in your life in general.

You can strengthen your sense of confidence by experiencing the growth and joy of musical involvement. Music, whether you listen to it or play it, brings challenges into your life that are fun and exciting to master. As you develop your listening skills, you become part of the community of music listeners who can fully hear and understand the glory of music, and grow emotionally from this source of enrichment. As a music-maker, your level of confidence rises sharply with each passage that you play or sing to your satisfaction.

• Listening to Build Confidence

In Chapter 8 we explained how you can come to know and understand yourself better through listening to music. By becoming acquainted with your reactions to the rhythms, melodies, and harmonies of a piece, you can learn about your means of coping with the rhythms, melodies, and harmonies that surround you in everyday life. And this added knowledge and acceptance of yourself serves to strengthen your identity as a person and to increase your self-esteem.

Your sense of confidence can also be increased through active listening. An editor at a New York City publishing house tells about how she discovered music while going through a painful divorce:

> I started listening to rock and roll almost by accident. But the more I listened, the more turned on to it I got. Suddenly I found myself wanting to buy records for the first time in my life, and wanting to find out more about specific artists and their songs. Because of my newly found interest, I eventually got to the point where I was able to recognize an artist by the sound of his music, or know when a musician had borrowed a guitar riff from another artist.
>
> What's exciting is that without even meaning to I've discovered a whole new body of knowledge that I never thought was open to me, because I was the one who "didn't have an ear for music." This has made me feel much more confident in general, and has made me realize that there are other areas that I can explore and get involved in that would make me happy.

When you open your ears to music in a new way, you begin to hear what music is really all about. Instead of hearing a blur of pleasant sound, you begin to know melodies well enough to recognize them in other settings or performed by a different artist. The melody becomes a part of you and is there for you to sing, hum, or whistle whenever you wish. You begin to recognize the rhythmic patterns well enough to tap them as you listen. You become familiar with different artists and their interpretations, and can recognize and know the qualities of the different instruments you hear. Aside from feeling increased confidence as a result of knowing more about music, through repeated listening you can experience more in the music, be touched more by the range of emotion that the music represents, and share more deeply in the communication that results when you actively listen to music with others.

Knowing about music is different from knowing about other art forms, hobbies, or interests. Music is an active part of our lives at all times. It is extremely rare to go through a day and not hear music. Unless you purposefully stay indoors all day and unplug your TV and radio, you are bound to hear background music as you shop, top-40 hits from kids on the street, or commercial jingles as you wait for the news to come on at night. If you remove yourself from music, you remove yourself from life itself. It's impossible to shut out music the way that we can close our eyes or cover our mouths. We were not meant to close ourselves off from music.

Becoming more familiar with this powerful accompaniment to daily living means knowing more about the culture and society in which you live, and about an art form that people respond to all day with their hearts, minds, bodies, and spirits. People love to talk about music! It's a topic about which everyone has something to say.

By becoming an active music listener, then, you gain skills that can not only enrich your internal life but also provide you with new options for social contact. The knowledge that you have these skills and the enjoyment you can derive from them boost your self-confidence, which in turn contributes to your growing sense of self-esteem.

Here are some ways to begin learning more about music in order to build your self-confidence:

1. *Let yourself fully contact the music you listen to.* Become an active music listener, as described in Chapter 8. This means that you listen, wholly undistracted, until you hear and feel your reaction to the interplay of melodies, rhythms, and harmonies. Take the time to listen to the same piece several times in order to do this.

Frederick S. Perls, who developed Gestalt therapy, and his colleagues have outlined an excellent means of listening that promotes greater awareness of music and of the self:

[A]bstract first the appearances of a single instrument. Then pay attention to the rhythm only; the timbre only. Detect what seems to be the melody, and what the accompaniment. Often you will find that there are other "inner melodies" that you had not expected. Abstract the harmony as you feel it; that is, notice when the harmony seems unresolved, seems to call for something more to come after it, and when, on the contrary, it seems to resolve and "close." Provided you do this seriously, suddenly all music will come alive for you.[1]

You can transfer the awareness you develop through active listening so as to enjoy a fuller, richer existence. Contact with friends can become deeper and more meaningful as you become aware of your feelings and sensations in the moments you are together. Your work, too, can become more meaningful as you become aware of aspects of your job you hadn't paid attention to before. By developing awareness in one area of your life, you can easily develop it in others. As an example, look around the room immediately after finishing this listening exercise. Pay attention to each object your eyes meet. Look at the texture, the line, the size. Contact the object fully, really *see* it before moving on to the next.[2] Your visual skills can follow the same route as your developing listening skills. By doing these exercises, expanding your senses, you can more fully experience and appreciate life, and meet its challenges with confidence. Music is the most accessible and available resource with which to build these skills.

2. *When listening to the radio, pay attention to artists' names and begin to connect them to the music you hear.* This will enhance your music experience. As you appreciate a particular singer's vocal quality, for example, you bring more enjoyment to your listening, and broaden your familiarity with different types of singers and, therefore, with different artistic styles. Similarly, listen for the names of the composers of the music you hear so that you can become familiar with their style and recognize other works by them.

3. *Read about music.* Read about upcoming record releases. Read concert reviews and interviews with musicians and composers. Read about the history of the kind of music you enjoy the most. There are scores of interesting books available on all aspects, styles, and forms of music.

4. *Listen to radio programs that include information about the music played.* Sometimes lectures are aired, as are live interviews with composers and recording artists.

5. *Attend live concerts.* Watch *how* musicians make music.

6. *Share your musical knowledge with others and learn from what they know.* Attending a concert with someone who is a fan

of the artist can be an especially pleasant and rewarding experience. You can also meet new people who share your wish to grow through music.

Remember—there is always more to learn about and to experience as a music listener. With more knowledge, you add to your appreciation of music, and with full music appreciation, you can build a sense of confidence throughout your life.

• Making Music to Build Confidence

Confidence is the result of mastery and skill-building. We feel confident when we feel strong, and know deep down that we can do what we set out to accomplish. Confidence involves practice and is often the result of successful past experiences.

Playing a musical instrument, voice included, can be an ideal means of developing confidence. When you set up a positive learning environment, music-making can be a path to tremendous growth. By this we mean that you study with a supportive teacher, a nurturing friend or group, or, if necessary, by yourself, but with the tools to create a positive experience. You will learn how to do this in Chapters 11 and 12.

A positive learning environment is also one in which you choose music that you enjoy and that is not too far beyond your skill level or vocal range. In order to develop confidence through music-making, you must arrange an environment geared for success.

Many of you may recall uncomfortable, even painful experiences you had learning music as a child. You may even have negative associations with certain instruments or certain pieces of music because of these unfortunate experiences. Such feelings are shared by many and are understandable. Many of us were forced to study with teachers who didn't understand the needs of children and who were unnecessarily strict and punitive. We were often made to play music we didn't appreciate, while being denied the opportunity to learn the music we would naturally choose to play. Practicing was monotonous and often took the place of needed playtime with friends. This is not true for *all* young music learners, of course. Many people were lucky enough to have studied with interesting and interested teachers, who provided nurturance as well as guidance.

If you had negative music-making experiences as a child, remember that *times have changed.* As an adult you can choose what, how, why, when, and where you wish to make music. You can fully enjoy the emotional and physical benefits of music-making on your own terms. Instead of boredom, you can experience excitement and inspiration. Instead of discomfort and embarrassment, you can experience joy, self-assurance, and confidence.

The unique confidence-building gift in music is that you can play or sing over and over again any passage or piece of music that you love. Once you learn a song, it's yours to create and re-create forever. With each repetition comes the knowledge that:

- You are an expressive person.
- You have developed musical skills.
- You can use these skills to bring relaxation, joy, and excitement into your life whenever you wish.
- You can actively participate in an art form that has always been a part of history, culture, and life itself.

Each successful rendering of a piece of music lets you know that "you can do it." Confidence grows with the familiarity, the repetition, the joy, and the accomplishment of music-making. The more music you can play, the more confidence you gain.

Practicing is the key to the mastery that builds confidence. When we say "practicing," we are *not* referring to the meaningless exercises you may have been forced to do as a child. Practicing can be fun, creative, and integrating. Of course, there will be times when you'll tire of practicing, but these can be the exceptions rather than the rule. When you practice music that you *choose* to play or sing, and when you are motivated and determined to play that piece of music well, practice sessions can be times of mental, physical, and emotional challenge and stimulation. Seymour Bernstein, well-known pianist, teacher, and author, writes the following about practice on his instrument:

Productive practicing is a process that promotes self-integration. It is the kind of practicing that puts you in touch with an all-pervasive order—an order that creates a total synthesis of your emotions, reason, sensory perceptions, and physical coordination. The result is an integration that builds your self-confidence and affirms the unification of you and your talent.[3]

We will tell you exactly how to practice in a pleasurable and productive manner in Chapter 11. Once you have developed these skills, here are some ways to continue building your self-confidence through making music:

1. *Develop a repertoire.* Once you have mastered a piece of music, hold on to it. Play it every so often so that you can continue to physically perform it. As you learn more music, you'll have built up a repertoire of pieces to play or sing for yourself and others.

2. *Choose music appropriate to your skill level.* There is material available for beginning, intermediate, and advanced music-makers, in all styles of music. If you choose pieces that are too difficult, you'll become frustrated and won't be able to enjoy the music. If, on the other hand, the pieces you choose are too easy, you won't benefit from musical challenge and won't gain the sense of accomplishment that comes from working toward mastery on your instrument.

3. *Learn different types of music.* By being able to play or sing a variety of pieces, you can better suit your many moods; and, if you wish, you'll be able to play at a variety of occasions.

4. *Every once in a while, do choose easy music to read through as part of your practice time.* By doing so, you can get a sense of your musical growth, receive instant gratification as you enjoy the music, and, at the same time, broaden your repertoire.

5. *Play the music you love most.* Play the music that makes you *feel* more confident. If you sing, choose songs that tell of growth, self-respect, and strength.

6. *Whenever possible, play for nurturing friends, roommates, a lover, or family members.* Being listened to, and feeling heard and responded to, is one of our most primitive needs. When someone listens to us, we feel stroked and cared for. Making music for others is a way to meet these needs and provide enjoyment for the listener as well. No matter how little music you can play, let yourself enjoy your sounds as you proudly show them off. Your attitude about your music-making can be contagious.

Listen to music in a new way, and learn about this fantastic, magical art form. Become a part of the experience, and listen to

the sounds you can create. Watch your hands execute passages
written by musical geniuses born hundreds of years ago, and enjoy
this sense of mastery and accomplishment over and over again
as you perform your repertoire for yourself and/or others. Music
is a direct line to the self. It can provide access to our innermost
resources and help us develop skills in a pleasurable, exciting
way. Let yourself join in this process, and develop your self-confidence with music.

10

Music for Closer Communication

M usic is communication, and communication is music.[1] Beginning with our first cry at birth, we use sound to express our presence, our needs, our desires, our joys, and our sorrows. We learn to recognize others' feelings and needs as well by the sounds they make. As described in Chapter 1, it is primarily through sound that we ensure survival in our earliest years of life.

By making and receiving sound as infants, we are also making and receiving love. The wordless, musical communication that takes place between mother and infant is profound, and pure, and is the expression of the exquisite intimacy of the relationship. As we grow up, it is music that helps us re-create and experience the deep satisfaction of sharing intimacy.

Music fosters bonding in relationships. As children sing together while they play, they share the joy of discovery and friendship in new ways. Songs take on secret shared meanings within certain young friendships—sometimes silly, sometimes dirty, often explorative, and always fun. Camp songs and chants encourage group expression and communication, and provide the satisfaction of shared group experience. In some camps, each bunk has its own song, giving that small group a sense of identity and cohesiveness.

Songs sung while traveling with the family become associated with adventure, vacation, and a sense of family closeness. Think back. . . . Did you have any family songs that made the time fly in seemingly endless car rides to the mountains, to the beach, or to visits with relatives and friends? If so, these songs will probably elicit memories and trigger the feelings that accompanied them for the rest of your life.

As adolescents, we imbue music with tremendous meaning. Certain songs "speak" to us and help us experience our deepest feelings. Faster rhythms attract us as our bodily rhythms accelerate. Dancing to rhythmic music becomes a way of releasing sexual tension and of communicating with the opposite sex. During this phase of life, music helps us become aware of and join the society that exists outside of home and school. We follow the careers of our favorite artists, attend concerts, and allow ourselves to dream about what other ways of living may be like. Music provides a safe way to identify with others during this often dissonant period. The music defines our likes, dislikes, physical appearance, mood, and means of expression; most important, it fosters close communication with our peers, giving us a feeling of belonging and purpose.

During this time, and throughout the rest of our lives, music continues to be an expression of love. Think back to your first romantic relationship. What was "your song"? What did the song mean to you, and what happened when you and your partner heard it together? What do you feel and remember when you hear that song now? One of the most poignant gifts of music is its ability to elicit the most tender emotions. In this way it communicates directly to our hearts and souls, and helps us share these private feelings with those we love.

Consider the lyrics of most music heard on the radio today. The topics, almost one hundred percent of the time, are about love, intimate relationships, and feelings. These involve sentiments that cannot be expressed in words alone. They are communicated through our eyes, through our bodies, and through the flowing tension and release in the music experience. The combination of music and lyrics stimulates romanticism and passion. You may be one of the many who enjoy listening to music while making love. Some feel that music "turns up the volume" on the emotions, adding to the lovemaking experience.

Another potent function of music in our lives is that it helps us communicate with meaningful experiences and feelings from our past, particular melodies evoking particular memories. Think of what happens to you when you hear a song from a while back. You can most likely identify the time in your life when you first heard it, picture who you were with, and remember how you felt as you heard the song. Experiencing this can be extremely self-affirming in helping you to realize the fullness and depth of your life.

The meaning music has for us as an access to memories and feelings increases with the years. Music therapists who work with ailing senior citizens use the songs of different eras to call up these old memories, supplying intellectual, emotional, spiritual, and physical stimulation for patients who are otherwise uncommunicative and unmotivated. Through familiar songs these persons can relive feelings of their past, which helps them to come alive in the present. Music is the bridge between eras, persons, and even seemingly unreachable parts of the self.

Although words are a most useful tool in communicating our thoughts to others, they are inadequate when it comes to expressing the depth, intensity, and scope of feeling of which we are capable. Imagine trying to describe a smile, a hug, or a tearful eye with words alone! Nonverbal communication provides a language without which we are expressionless.

Have you ever tried to describe to someone else a piece of music that touched you deeply? After several attempts to define the experience, you probably gave up and said, "You just have to hear it!" The music speaks for us, to us, and within us. As Felix Mendelssohn astutely observed, music "is not too vague, but too precise for words."[2]

How does music possess this quality? Researchers, philosophers, psychologists, and other scholars have been pondering this question since the beginning of time. Susanne Langer, a philosopher renowned for her contributions in the field of aesthetics, claims that music exists in a dynamic form that moves through time, as do our feelings. Both music and feelings ebb and flow, intensify and diminish, and embody motion, rest, and sudden change. Both music and feelings exist only as long as the flow of movement continues. A visual parallel would be a waterfall. The waterfall exists only as long as the water flows. It is the movement that defines the form of the waterfall, of our feelings, and of music.[3]

It is because both emotions and music move similarly through time that we respond so strongly to music with feeling, and we express feeling in our music. Static forms simply do not evoke the same type of response as does music. Growing trees, flowers, and other natural phenomena often do, because they are in motion, even though the movement may be microscopic.

According to Langer, the purpose of all art is to express human feeling. And music, a language of emotions, is created by man in order to understand his internal life. Simply stated, the music sounds the way feelings feel.[4] The reason that we create music is to understand our feelings, to express them deeply, and to communicate them to others.

Another reason why music is hard to describe in words, and is so revealing of our emotional states, may derive from its role in our preverbal existence. As described in Chapter 3, before we had words, we had music. We had the rhythms of our mother's body surrounding us *in utero,* and made our own sounds—crying, gurgling, cooing—as infants and toddlers, and were comforted and soothed by rocking, soft murmurings, and songs.

During these stages of life, we had no words to describe our experience; all we knew was that the musical interactions we had felt good. Our situation with music is similar today, as adults. Music still satisfies our needs for gratification and nurturance, and although we can now use language, we remain at a loss for words when attempting to describe what music sounds like, feels like, and does for us. Most of us find it enough to say "I can't describe it. Music just makes me feel good." It's as if music brings us back to a time of nonverbal satisfaction and peace, where words are unnecessary for true understanding. The music says it all.

If you have ever sung songs amid a group of people, chosen suitable music to be played at a social gathering, played music with others, or listened to a favorite album with a friend, you have already used music as a powerful communicative tool in your life. By continuing to use music in this manner, you can expand your repertoire of expression with yourself and others. Peak experiences, which were described in Chapter 7, are often the result of these types of nonverbal communication exchanges. Such experiences usually stem from and result in a feeling of becoming one with the world, of feeling connected, and of feeling whole.

There are several means by which you can increase your expression and communication with others through listening to music, singing, and playing an instrument. Here are some ways to begin.

• Listening to Music for Communication

1. *Take the time to listen to music with someone special.* Don't use the music as background for another activity. Relax together, actively listen, and immerse yourselves in the sounds.

Exercise 10-1

The purpose of this exercise is for you to feel that you are sharing a common experience with your friend. You may not feel the same way about the music you hear, and may have different internal reactions as you listen. This doesn't matter and need not detract from the exercise.

To begin, sit near each other (holding hands if you wish), close your eyes, and listen. Let your mind and body react to the rhythm, melody, and harmony. Be aware of who you're listening with. Ask yourself the following questions:

- How do you feel as you listen to the music?
- What is it like to listen to this music with this person?
- Do you want to do anything together as you listen? Dance? Sing? Hug? Make love?

When the music ends, take turns sharing your feelings and reactions with each other. Are they the same or different? Did you feel a bond between you, wondering how the other was feeling? If you were holding hands, what did you feel in each other's hand as you listened? How did this help you communicate?

Listening to music with a friend, lover, or spouse can be a relaxing way to communicate deep feelings with each other without the interference of words. Sitting quietly, you can share the experience of receiving a composer's message in a private musical moment together.

Try Exercise 10-1 with music you've never heard before, as well as with old favorites or "your song."

2. *Attend a concert with a friend.* Follow the directions for Exercise 10-1, but feel the difference in intensity that comes from listening to live music. Communication is enhanced in every way. The

artist is there to communicate to you and you are there to receive the music, as well as to communicate your reactions to him. You communicate with your friend, sharing feelings about what you're hearing, as well as simply being part of a potent musical experience together.

Another of music's special gifts is that when listening to music with others, there's room for everyone to have a mutual, as well as an individual, musical experience. One hundred people can attend a concert and each sense the music differently. They are each, however, part of a group who have shared a common creative evening together.

Peak experiences often come about when music is felt by many listeners in the same way. In other cultures, mostly Eastern, drumming and chanting frequently accompany religious rites and rituals. The music helps propel those present into a state of ecstacy and trance, culminating in a shared peak experience that reaffirms religious beliefs and practice. In this country, beautiful renditions of classical masterworks have been known to affect entire audiences so deeply that prolonged, stunned silences precede applause when the music is over. The powerful communication that takes place between artist, audience, and composer is enriching and rewarding to all who are present in the musical moment.

3. *Use songs to communicate feelings to others.* Radio shows often allow listeners to call in and dedicate a song to someone special. If you have ever had a song dedicated to you, you know that the combination of music and words can serve as a powerful means of communication between two persons. The person dedicating the song has a strong message to relate and, through the right piece of music, can communicate his feelings and thoughts directly to the other.

If you have something special to say to someone, let music help you get your message across. As well as expressing your feelings verbally as best you can, give that person a gift of a special song to listen to. "Dedicate" it to him or her in your own way. Let the music carry your message straight to your friend's heart.

Don't reserve this treat only for romantic relationships. A song makes a wonderful gift for any friend, as a mid-week pick-me-up or to celebrate a special moment. Make a special song part

of your next mother's- or father's-day present and listen to it together. Instead of struggling with a card inscription, let the music
speak for you.

Use songs to communicate with friends or relatives who are
far away. You can choose songs to describe what's going on in
your life, your mood, how you feel about their being away, and
how you look forward to seeing them. You can include songs
that may describe their situations as well. Send the music either
on cassette or record, or simply mention, on a card or over the
phone, the title of a particular song that you would like them to
hear.

Don't forget to occasionally dedicate a song to yourself. When
you need extra support and love in your life, find a song that
tells you what you need to hear in order to more easily make it
through the uncomfortable period. If, for example, you're starting
a new job and feel a little nervous and insecure, listen to a song
that communicates confidence, vigor, and success. This can help
you gear up for a positive experience at work. Whatever the situation, there is a song to help you understand it and get through
it. Let the piece become your theme song for a while as you
gain strength from its message.

• Making Music For Communication

SINGING:

The voice is our most powerful communicative tool and one
that expresses personality with each sound we produce. Singing
is a way to express our most profound feelings to ourselves and
to others. At a campfire, party, or concert, we sing together to
have fun, create a mood, share a common experience, and communicate who we are to those around us. By singing in a group,
you experience the whole as well as its parts. You hear your voice,
the individual qualities of the voices nearest you, and the harmonious blend of the group. You express yourself through your style
of singing, the intensity of your voice, the harmonies you add,
and the meaning you impart to the music. The experience is aesthetically pleasing, and you can feel the joy of communicating
this pleasure with others.

Here are some ways to bring these benefits into your life through
singing with others:

1. *Create or establish family songs and participate in songs sung around the campfire or at social gatherings.*
2. *Attend a concert that encourages group participation.* This is a wonderful way for you to experience your vocal expression in a group. Folk concerts abound where well-known songs are sung and shared by all. Holiday seasons are especially popular times to catch these concerts. Since everyone goes there to sing, there is a general feeling of permission to let go of the fears, inhibitions, and embarrassment that often accompany the singing experience. Singing a favorite song with hundreds of others can be a thrilling experience.

Houses of worship provide another source of group singing that is nonpressuring, pleasurable, and meaningful. If you attend a service, let the music you sing connect you with your community of fellow worshipers, as well as with the religious experience.

3. *Sing with a friend.* As a youngster, you probably spent time with your buddies singing the popular songs of the era, communicating your feelings of friendship to one another and to those around you. Let yourself sing with someone who's close to you now, as an adult. Try spending a few minutes by the fire on a chilly evening, taking a trip in the car, or sunning on the beach singing together songs that are meaningful to you. You will probably have a surprisingly enjoyable experience.

Singing is not like other activities done with friends; it is a shared intimate expression of yourself. While fun and emotionally satisfying, singing with a friend can bring the two of you much closer. Depending on the songs you choose—their lyrics and style—you will learn more about each other's personality, likes, dislikes, mood, etc. Sharing the type of music you like with others, and singing it with or for them, is a powerful way to communicate who you are to those you love.

PLAYING AN INSTRUMENT:

Your musical instrument is an extension of yourself. It helps you express your deepest feelings in the meaningful language of music. When you make sounds, they touch those around you and call for a response. By making music in the presence of others, you initiate a nonverbal conversation that can be a most rewarding source of gratification. Here are some ways to develop your communication and expression through playing an instrument:

1. *If there is a piece that you feel good about playing, play it for someone you care about and trust.* Let yourself experience the music and share yourself through the music with your listener.

When you finish, you may wish to play the piece again immediately. Many of us are nervous the first time we play for someone, and don't get a chance to enjoy the music. Play it again and this time let yourself enjoy your artistry as you communicate with your listener.

Afterward, ask your friend to share her thoughts and feelings with you about what she heard and also what she learned about you through your music. You will be surprised at what even an inexperienced music listener can learn about a person from listening to your music. For example, did she find you expressive? Bold? Musical? Romantic? Could she tell, by listening, that it was you playing? What did she feel that you communicated through the music?

You can create another level of relationship when you share your music with someone. The same is true when you are the listener. Make sure that you experience the other side of this exercise. Seek out a friend whose music you would like to hear and share your feedback with him.

2. *Create music with a friend.* This may seem like an impossible feat, but it is not. It is actually quite simple. In Chapter 6 we showed you some easy ways to begin improvising on the piano. We explained how with only five notes on the piano and only five fingers, you can begin to create melodies on your own. This is an exercise that is fun, expressive, and communicative when done with a friend:

Exercise 10-2

Find the same set of five adjacent white notes in two different places on the keyboard. The notes will sound the same, but one set will be higher, and one set lower. You will know if you have the same set of notes by looking at their relation to the black keys above them. While the white keys stretch out over the whole keyboard, the black keys are grouped in twos and threes.

Look to see whether your set of white notes begins near a set of three black notes or two. Then find the same spot somewhere else on the piano. Each of you will be playing one set of notes. Make sure that you like your choice of notes. Each group of five notes on the keyboard will make a completely different sound. Take the time to experiment and find a group whose sound is attractive to both of you.

The point of this exercise is to have a musical conversation. When you're both ready, one of you can begin by playing a short melody. The other person will answer with his own. Let the conversation continue naturally, and let yourselves communicate with each other through the music. Punctuate your statements by playing some notes louder or shorter. Emphasize your meaning by mixing strong, definite sounds. Can you be cajoling? Funny? Redundant? Irritating? Do you listen fully to your partner's statements or tend to interrupt?

Let the conversation last as long as is comfortable, and observe how it closes. Does it end naturally, seemingly by itself, or do you need to consciously finish it? When you've stopped, share your thoughts, feelings, and perceptions with each other. How was this conversation similar to or different from verbal conversations you have had together? Did you learn anything about each other by doing this? Do you feel that you communicated with each other through your music? Try this exercise again with a different set of notes and see what happens.

Exercise 10-3

Another way to communicate while improvising is to play simultaneously instead of in conversation. Locate two new sets of white notes (again, the same sets but in different registers of the piano) and begin playing together.

Let yourself create melodies, and develop a give and take in the music. Feel yourself in communication with your friend's musical expression. Let the music continue to rise and fall naturally as you continue to play.

Did you feel in sync with his rhythms, or did you want to play faster or slower? Did you feel less or more expressive than he? Did you feel his presence in the music?

The answers to these questions can reveal a lot about your relationship with this person in general. For instance, are your daily rhythms different? Does he move too fast or too slow for you? Does this dissonance cause friction between you when you're together? Or are your rhythms well matched and satisfying?

Your musical communication can highlight the interpersonal dynamics of your verbal conversations and relationship with this person. Be aware, also, of the heightened communication that can take place when making music that doesn't occur during verbal conversation. What was special to you about the musical interchanges you had with your friend?

Here are some variations on these two exercises:

A. Try both exercises—playing in conversation and simultaneously—with each of you playing different sets of notes, rather than the same ones. Again, make sure that you locate two sets whose sounds are appealing to you. Take the time to explore the keyboard to find sounds that go well together. Let your ears lead the way.

B. Try a set of eight adjacent white notes, rather than five. An eight-note set is called an "octave" and is a common musical unit. The first and eighth notes you play will sound similar, but the first will sound lower than the eighth. These two notes would be called by the same name. If the first was a "C," the eighth would be called "C" as well.

When you play the notes one by one from the first C to the second, you are playing a scale—in this case, a C scale. The sound this produces is probably familiar to you, for it is a common scale in Western music. You may associate this sound with children's songs and songs from your youth. Try improvising music together on other scales, such as those beginning on D, G, and E. What is the difference in the sound to you? Does the different sound of the scale influence your communication with each other?

C. Try adding a black note here and there, as suggested in the earlier improvisation exercises.

D. If you or your friend play other instruments, locate similar groups of notes on them, and try both exercises. Try also to freely improvise, without any structure, on these instruments. Let yourself create melodies and rhythms, and feel the interplay between you.

E. If you don't play a traditional instrument, you can still do these musical-communication exercises with a friend. Try using two pots, stamping your feet, blowing into empty bottles, or clapping your hands. There are musical resources all around you.

3. *Experience the joy of playing duets.* There are scores of piano duets for four hands, written for pianists of different skill levels. If you are a string or woodwind player, seek out a pianist and choose sonatas or other appropriate pieces to play together. Browse in your local music store for different duets you could play with others, and ask the clerk or your teacher for help in deciding which music would be right for you.

Experiencing the music process with another person is extremely rewarding. You can build a repertoire of expression with each other that can enhance an established friendship or help form a close, new one.

4. *Play chamber music.* If you have had a few years' experience on an orchestral instrument, piano included, you may be able to participate in one of the most powerful communicative musical experiences.

In chamber music, one player plays each musical line, as opposed to orchestral music, where many instrumentalists share each part. Chamber groups generally vary in size from three to eight players and are usually comprised of string instruments, woodwinds, and the piano, in varying combinations.

The pleasure derived from playing chamber music is immense. Often musicians who have played with orchestras all over the world and have done numerous solo concerts report that their greatest delight lies in playing chamber music with others of equal talent. There is joy in being able to expressively carry a musical line on one's own and create freely within the structure of the written notes. The greatest thrill, however, comes from the heightened communication that takes place among the players. The intimate relationships expressed through the sound, the flow between group and individual musical statements, and the nuances understood only by the participants create a unique environment. For the duration of the piece, the members of the chamber group exist as one in a world composed of beautiful sound and flowing feelings.

Throughout the United States, instrumentalists seek out chamber groups in order to have this experience, and balance the sense of aloneness that can come from always making music by oneself. The desire to play with others is a common bond among musicians. For this reason, more chamber music continues to be written and arranged for more diverse instruments and for varying levels of musical talent.

In order for genuine communication to take place, there must be contact and withdrawal. Contact is the result of the meeting of one separate identity with another. It involves a sense of the self, as well as a sense of who is being contacted.[5] In the moment of true contact, these two separate entities meet and merge, and experience their union. In healthy relationships, a natural withdrawal takes place afterward, during which the two selves separate and re-establish their distinct identities.

Through experiencing this contact-and-withdrawal cycle we strengthen our identities, as well as engage in true deep communication with others. Intimacy becomes a reality, and loneliness an increasingly unfamiliar feeling.

Because music is a form of communication, contact is made whenever the music process is fully experienced. When listening to music with another person, you share a level of contact as you are simultaneously affected by the music. An extremely deep level of contact can be experienced when one is actively making music with others. This is why such elation is often felt in the musical encounter. Contact is essential in our lives, and when true contact occurs, we can feel joyous, vibrant, and appreciative of both ourselves and others. Music, by nature, promotes contact, communication, and the heightened emotions that flow from intimacy with those around us. By bringing more music into your life, you can experience the benefits of close communication and meaningful contact with yourself, your family, and your friends.

Creativity, joy, self-esteem, confidence, and communication are all separate human properties, yet are connected. Each one can directly affect the development of the other, and when there is growth in one area, there tends to be growth in the others as well. For example, when improvising music with another person, you are creating music, which is most often a joyous process. By contacting the other person through the music, you raise the level of communication between you, energizing both your connectedness and your separateness as individuals. This, plus your awareness of your ability to create music in the moment, can bolster your sense of self-esteem and contribute to your developing confidence in music-making, social activities, and improvising in other areas of your life.

Music is one of the most powerful human resources available to everyone, regardless of age, religion, race, sex, or economic status. It can be made naturally with our voices, hands, and feet or with the help of well-designed musical instruments. It can be given or received. Although it is always a source of entertainment, it is also a source of human growth and development. As you bring more music into your life, you will probably realize that there are many more than five ways that music can help you make changes. More discoveries about how music can enhance your life lie ahead in the following chapters.

III
Making Music: A Guide for the Adult Beginner

Argue for your limitations,
and sure enough,
they're yours.
    —Richard Bach

11

Playing an Instrument

When you think about making music, do you believe one or more of the following statements?

1. "I'm too old to learn how to play an instrument."
2. "I'm not musical. I have no musical talent and could never learn to play."
3. "I could never find the time to practice."
4. "It would be too expensive. I can't afford to learn how to play."
5. "I could never be great, so it doesn't pay for me to learn at all."
6. "I have no right to play an instrument. My sister was the musical one in the family."

These are the more popular myths that have been created about music-making. *Not one of them is true.* If you have believed one or more of these myths for most of your life, you have been misinformed. By understanding the truth about your ability to play an instrument, you can join the world of enthusiastic music-makers and experience the benefits that music-making can bring into your life.

Myth 1: "I'm too old to learn how to play an instrument."
You can *never* be too old to learn how to play an instrument. Although our capacity for learning is greatest when we are very young, it does not necessarily continue to diminish steadily as we get older. A recent research study of normal, elderly, white women revealed that there is no significant decrease of musical

ability with age. These women were able to maintain and even improve their musical skills when they wished.[1] Many people learn new hobbies, such as knitting, sewing, or cooking, at a later age. Music-making is no different.

Music can even help you feel younger. Many people report feeling more invigorated after playing. Practicing rhythmic music can trigger a physical response that improves circulation and helps you feel more energetic. Slower, more melodious music can help you feel relaxed and calm when you need to. Filling your lungs with air to sing or to play a woodwind instrument can help you breathe more deeply,* and the improved posture and physical movement that come with practice can lead to a fulfilling sense of integration and joy.

So, instead of sticking to the belief that you're too old to learn or relearn how to play an instrument, why not bring into your life music that will energize you and help you feel good about your age? If there is an instrument you have always wanted to play, *now* is the time to learn.

Myth 2: "I'm not musical. I have no musical talent and could never learn to play."

While reading the first chapter of this book, you learned that by nature of the fact that you are human, you are musical. As an infant and a toddler you called for attention by making sound, learned to speak through singing, and enjoyed a wide variety of sound-making activities. As an adult, you are rhythmic in your step and your pulse, melodious in the use of your voice, and harmonious in your social behavior. Further evidence of your musical nature lies in your appreciation of the music you listen to. You may respond by tapping along, by humming or singing, or simply by experiencing a change of mood or a rush of emotion as you hear the music you love. Each reaction is proof of your native musical abilities.

You do not need to have musical talent in order to play an instrument. Talent plays a part in the level of music you can play and the special way your body may be able to coax sound from an instrument. But if you can breathe, move your fingers, use

---

* Instruments that demand breath control may be difficult if you have a medical condition associated with the lungs. Consult your doctor before making your instrument choice.

your voice, and tap in rhythm to a song, you already have several skills necessary to play an instrument. Even if the last three skills are difficult for you, there are instruments that can be adapted for your use. Playing an instrument is something that everyone can do. You may never become a professional, but you can learn to play for your enjoyment and to enhance your physical and emotional well-being.

"Anyone can be taught the physical mechanics of playing an instrument," says Edward Lewis, associate professor of music at the University of Regina, Saskatchewan. Lewis is a professional trumpet player and has been teaching trumpet students for twenty-five years.

> When my students complain that they don't have the talent to succeed on their instrument, I often draw an analogy to athletics. Some persons possess an unusual amount of natural ability and drive, which contributes to their careers as tennis players. Millions of others, however, play tennis as a fun sport and source of exercise, and enjoy the game regardless of their amateur status. Music-making is no different in this respect. Anyone can develop their own skills and abilities. The only limit is one's own mental set.

Some instruments are more difficult to learn than others. If you are determined, however, you will be able to play the one you want. Interest, determination, and love for music are much more important than talent when it comes to learning how to play.

Myth 3: "I could never find the time to practice."

In order to get started as a music-maker and maintain a basic level of skill, you will need to devote only about twenty minutes a day to playing and practicing. *This is, of course, a minimum.* The more time you can devote to your music-making, the faster you'll progress. However, if you manage a job, a family, school, or a combination of these, you need not feel that you must practice hours every day. On the days when you have a full load, try taking twenty minutes in the morning, while the coffee's brewing, to work on your music. What a creative, integrating way to begin your day! Or, if the idea of anything but rolling out of bed and dashing off to work is alien to you, consider playing for a few minutes during your lunch break, if time and space allow. Music-making can be a wonderful way to re-energize yourself after a long morning at work.

Many people find that evenings are best for making music. Some play as soon as they get home, as a means of unwinding. Others wait until the mid or late evening, when the children are asleep, the dinner dishes are done, and it is possible to fully relax and enjoy the music.

If you are fortunate enough to create your own work schedule, it will be easy to find practice time during the day. In addition, weekends are a time when you will probably have the freedom to choose the right time of day for your music-making.

Since music-making is something you choose to do for yourself, don't berate yourself if you don't get to your instrument every day. There will be days when you really won't have time to play. However, remember that by making time for music, you also make time for yourself. When you claim practice time, no matter whether it's twenty minutes or two hours, that time is yours to learn, express, feel, relax, contact yourself, and entertain yourself. You deserve this time. The benefits can be tremendous.

Myth 4: "It would be too expensive. I can't afford to learn how to play."

Most of the time, playing an instrument does involve spending some money. However, you can find ways to make this cost as low as possible. You'll be spending money on three things: the instrument, a teacher (or study course, if necessary), and printed music.

• Acquiring an Instrument

You have some choices about how to spend money on an instrument. Buying an instrument can be relatively expensive. Renting an instrument can be relatively cheap. Borrowing an instrument until someone wonderful buys one for you costs nothing. You may be lucky enough to own an instrument already, or know of one in the family that no one is using. Investigate your options for acquiring an instrument in your neighborhood. If the local high school has an extra flute or saxophone in good repair, see if you can rent or borrow it for the year. Sometimes music stores carry good-quality instruments that are old or secondhand and that sell for much less than the price of a new one. Many teachers own an extra instrument they'll gladly lend to a student as an incentive for learning.

There *are* ways to get around the high cost of buying an instrument if you really don't have the funds. But try your best not to compromise on quality. The better the quality of the instrument, the better the sound you will be able to produce. This sound will have a direct impact on your self-esteem and confidence as you practice and advance your skills. You're worth a good instrument. It's important that you have the best musical experiences possible.

If you should come into money at some point, do buy yourself the best instrument possible. It will be an investment for life, and you deserve it.

• Acquiring a Teacher

The cost of a teacher depends on where you live and on the teacher's level of experience. Teachers in New York City sometimes charge up to three times more than teachers in small towns, and a conservatory faculty member will obviously charge much more for a lesson than a college music major. Ask around your community, in schools, and among your friends for the names of teachers who are good, who are supportive, and whose fee would fit into your price range. Just because a teacher charges a lot doesn't necessarily mean that she is good. The right teacher for you may not have as much experience as a Juilliard graduate but may be able to communicate a love for music in a way that touches you deeply. Remember that when you choose a teacher, you are hiring her for an important service. Interview a few people before you choose, and base your decision on how you feel with that person, as well as on the practical issues involved. Don't work with someone who seems disinterested, critical, or unaware of your needs. Music-making involves emotional expression, and it's essential for you to feel comfortable and enjoy sharing the music process with your teacher.

In some communities, teachers will barter with students for other services. If you have skills that others may be needing, such as knowledge of a foreign language, experience with legal issues, or the ability to easily complete and file income-tax forms, you may be able to find a teacher who will gladly exchange an hour's worth of your expertise for an hour of hers.

You can also adapt the cost of studying by taking a lesson every other week instead of every week, or by taking half-hour lessons. There may be some teachers who would agree to this arrangement, or might even find it favorable. If you can, however, it is best to study once a week for forty-five minutes or an hour. Frequent contact with your teacher helps keep your interest level high and can help you feel more satisfied with your progress. The weekly feedback and encouragement is extremely important for your musical and emotional growth.

There is another means of studying, which is not ideal but is extremely cost-effective. There are many different study courses available in music stores, which you can do on your own or with friends. Some of them come equipped with cassette tapes, so that you can associate what you're learning to read with what the music sounds like. Although many of these are designed for individual use, we suggest that you find a music-learning partner and work together. In this way you help keep each other's interest and motivation going, and you can have more fun in the process. You can encourage each other and be each other's audience. After a while you'll be able to play duets together and share a new level of communication and fun. Choose someone who is eager to learn, who will be fun to work with, and who will be willing to meet with you at a scheduled time each week. You can make the most of these musical evenings together by attending concerts after the study sessions, or by enjoying dinner together either before or after you play.

Remember that the ideal learning situation is one in which you have a terrific teacher to work with every week. A good friend and well-written materials can be an alternative, though, when money is a problem. You may also want to consider hiring a teacher to work with the two of you together. You can then benefit from her experience and divide the fee between you. Group sessions may also be an option.

• Acquiring Sheet Music

It is worth it for you to invest in your own copies of printed music. After all, when you study an instrument you become a trained musician, and all trained musicians own their own music. You will need to mark fingerings in pencil on your copy, and jot down expressive markings, comments, or suggestions from your teacher. Also, if you will be carrying the music around with you, you won't want to worry about someone else's copy going through the wear and tear. You may want to borrow pieces from your teacher to sight-read, but when you choose to learn a piece, it's best that you have your own copy.

Most persons spend between ten and twenty-five dollars on sheet music during their first year of study. This minimal fee is a lifelong investment. You will have the music forever, and be able to play the pieces whenever you wish.

Myth 5: "I could never be great, so it doesn't pay for me to learn at all."

If you feel this way about learning music, you probably feel similarly about other areas of your life. This is a "What's-the-use?" attitude, which can leave you feeling unfulfilled and unhappy. In Chapter 6 we told you about primary creativeness, which occurs in the moment and is not product-oriented. This sense of creating without having to produce is indigenous to us. It is what helped you learn and explore as a young child. As an adult, playing for your own satisfaction can increase your confidence and sense of self-esteem, and helps to bring more joy into your life. If you feel that you need to be the best in order to play at all, you may be trying to live up to the expectations of your parents or other authority figures of your youth. Think about it for a minute. If playing an instrument will bring you pleasure, and your goal is to bring more enrichment into your life, does it really matter how "good" you become? Of course you'll feel better about the sounds you create as your musical skills develop. This doesn't mean that you can't enjoy the *process* of learning and playing music. One musician we spoke with, who teaches in Massachusetts, feels that this attitude is essential. As she told us, "The music is already in our fingers and in our voices. If we can only remove the conscious 'trying-to-make-music-perfectly' part of ourselves, we can then be free to create."

By denying yourself the chance to play for fear that you won't excel, you are ruling out an avenue of great pleasure and growth in your life. Let yourself accept your level of music-making, no matter *what* it is. Remember, you will be doing this for you. You won't have your family or friends measuring your progress or expecting you to prove your excellence on your instrument as you may have when you were a child. Let yourself in on some of the fun available to you by becoming a music-maker!

Myth 6: "I have no right to play an instrument. My sister was the musical one in the family."

This is a common situation created by adoring parents. Instead of all the children in a family being able to have many traits at the same time, one becomes "the smart one," one "the good-looking one," and one "the creative one," et cetera. This attitude is based upon a feeling of scarcity, where it is imagined that there's not enough of a given trait, be it brains, talent, or beauty, to go around. Therefore, all three kids may feel that they can't be good-looking, smart, and musical at the same time, even though they may be. Each child receives a label that sticks for life. Once out of the family, the "creative" ones may feel that it is not their role to be smart, so they may never try to excel in school. And those who are "brainy" may feel that there's not room enough for them to enjoy music-making, too. This attitude breeds competition, as well as unnecessary feelings of failure and unhappiness.[2]

These labels are originally devised because children *do* demonstrate skills in certain areas as opposed to others. However, just because a child excels in science doesn't mean that she can't also play an instrument. By the same token, many gorgeous blondes are extremely bright, as opposed to the stereotype created in our society.

So, even if your sister was always known as "the musical one," there's room enough for you to step out of the musical background into your own music-making foreground. You can *both* make music. If she has had permission and encouragement to study music from a young age, she will probably have advanced skills. Don't let that make you feel bad. Let yourself be your own musi-

cian, with your own areas of strength and weakness. You deserve
to have the joys of music-making in your life.

• Giving Yourself Permission to Play

If playing an instrument seems scary to you, you are not alone.
There are reasons why music-making can be threatening and anxiety-producing. First of all, if you have had uncomfortable experiences playing an instrument in the past, it would make sense
that some of those feelings would carry over into the present.
Instead of being scared off by these memories, remember that
you are now in control of the music-making situation and can
create a positive learning environment for yourself.

The reason most people are scared of learning to play an instrument is that making music is self-revealing. Through the music
it is possible to contact and express feelings of which we are
usually unaware. Many people who are uncomfortable with experiencing these emotions stay away from music completely. Con-
versely, there are those who are attracted to music simply because
it is the one area in which they feel they *can* express emotion.
When you play an instrument, you make a statement about yourself, and this is scary for some people. They cringe at the thought
of others hearing their music, for fear of being judged. These
same people may also lack confidence when it comes to verbally
expressing their feelings. By looking at the fears you have about
playing an instrument, you can gain insight to the general feelings
you may have about yourself.

For example, what do you imagine would happen if you were
to take up playing an instrument? Think of both your positive
and negative expectations. You may feel that it would be a wonderful addition to your life, but that you could never keep it up. Is
this a general pattern for you? Are you usually a starter but not
a finisher? One of the gifts about making music is that if you
have the instrument and the music in your home, you are always
in the position to play. With the help of some of the guidelines
in this chapter, you may be able to change your usual pattern
and, instead, continue playing over a long period of time.

Do you imagine others being critical of or ridiculing your desire
to play? If this is a deterrant, stop and think. If you had a friend

who always wanted to make music and decided to take up an instrument, what would you think? Would you consider him strange or crazy? Or would you respect him, and even feel a little jealous that he got past the inertia of routine and boredom as he discovered a new source of excitement and growth? By going ahead and meeting your musical needs, you may be silently inviting your friends to make positive moves in their lives as well.

If the idea of expressing feeling in the music seems scary to you, remember that you were born having feelings, and these feelings are meant to be expressed. We often learn otherwise in our families. Let music help you get to know your deepest emotions. In order to be fully balanced and healthy, everyone needs a safe way to release tension and express feeling. As you play music of different eras, and music with different harmonies, melodies, and rhythms, you will experience a variety of feelings and moods. These are all a part of you. Instead of being scared by them, let yourself accept them, and celebrate *all* of who you are. By playing an instrument and listening to your sounds, you can experience yourself as a healthy, emotionally fulfilled person.

• The Benefits of Playing an Instrument

Music is a major source of gratification. Learning to play an instrument can be an especially potent means of experiencing this. Over seventy-five percent of the instrumentalists we questioned said that they gained a sense of accomplishment from playing their instrument, and over ninety percent reported that they experienced pleasure while making music. Joy, exhilaration, intellectual stimulation, and peace were also cited by more than half of those surveyed. One way to understand why music-making results in personal gratification is by looking at the learning process involved.

Abraham Maslow, whose ideas about creativity were discussed earlier, writes of two learning processes available to us—extrinsic and intrinsic. Extrinsic learning is that which is educationally required and extrinsically determined. Examples would be the courses required in an undergraduate curriculum, or the learning of safety rules as a child. While important, this type of learning usually does not make an impact on one's sense of self or change one as a person. Intrinsic learning, on the other hand, involves learning to be a human being. This learning takes place as a result of significant life experiences, such as involvement in meaningful relationships, having children, determining career choices, or making personal changes. Through intrinsic learning, one becomes more aware of who he really is.[3]

According to Clive Robbins, a pioneer in the field of music therapy, learning to play music most often begins as an extrinsic learning process but results in intrinsic learning. Initially, we take in technical information about the notes we're reading, their duration, and the tempo of the piece. We work on developing the skills necessary to play the instrument. As we play, however, we process the music, and emotions, thoughts, images, and physical sensations are triggered within us. We then begin feeling the benefits of musical involvement. We may acquire a new sense of ourselves as artists, gain confidence in our abilities, communicate more deeply with others (as well as with ourselves), and develop a joyous sense of our creative abilities. This intrinsic learning makes a tremendous impact on our continued internal growth, and brings us closer to meeting our need for self-actualization, or being the best person we can be. Music-making, therefore, can be a step toward health.[4]

Those benefits of playing a musical instrument which we have mentioned thus far include personal gratification, communication with others, increased confidence, and heightened sense of self-esteem. From surveying a number of instrumentalists in the New York area, we discovered many more ways people use their music-making to enhance their lives, and the benefits they experience as a result.

For example, approximately eighty percent of those we questioned played music to change their mood. A vast majority experienced an elevated mood as a result of playing their instrument. Other emotional changes reported by more than half of those questioned were heightened emotions, a sense of purpose, and increased creativity.

The physical benefits reported are noteworthy as well. Over seventy-five percent reported experiencing physical changes as a result of playing their instruments, with the most significant responses indicating a sense of physical well-being, improved eye-hand coordination, improved auditory acuity, improved manual dexterity, and physical relaxation.

Other significant data emerged in response to our questions

regarding the social benefits that can come from playing music with others. Over seventy-five percent said they experienced a sense of shared communication, enjoyment, personal recognition, and great satisfaction at finding such a pleasurable way to spend time with others.

For most of the persons surveyed, playing an instrument satisfied musical, as well as achievement, needs. For others, aesthetic, cultural, and financial needs were also satisfied by playing music alone or in a group.

The way in which you decide to make music will determine how many of these benefits you will actually experience from playing. The following is a guide to help you succeed in your growth as a music-maker and as a person.

• How to Succeed as a Music-Maker

The five necessary components for successful music-making are:

- A good instrument, with a sound that is pleasing to you.
- A positive learning environment, preferably with a good teacher.
- Practice time that is reasonable, challenging, and satisfying.
- Opportunities to share your music with those who are supportive and nurturing.
- Internal acceptance of ups and downs.

Let's talk about each of these individually:

A GOOD INSTRUMENT

The first two components were discussed in detail on pages 114–15 of this chapter, but remember that if you can't afford to buy a good instrument now, you can rent or borrow one until you can purchase your own. While you may not start off with the best instrument, if you begin to save a few dollars each week, you will soon be able to get an instrument of good, if not excellent, quality. A good-quality guitar, for example, can be bought new for as little as one hundred dollars.

A POSITIVE LEARNING ENVIRONMENT

Remember that a good music teacher can become a guide for you as you explore the world of music. He can provide you with knowledge of the lives of the composers and the history of the pieces you're playing. He can introduce you to works that are very popular, as well as to pieces that are rarely played but that may be suited to your taste. A good teacher does much more than help you read and translate the black dots and lines printed on the page. You can learn about the music, about the meaning of the sounds, and about *yourself.* Your teacher can help you appreciate your physical and emotional reactions to the music you play, and how your sounds are reflective of your individuality.

A teacher creates a positive learning environment when he can push you to practice when necessary, as well as accept where you are when you are at your most and least productive points. As opposed to what many of us learned as children, guilt is not a necessary motivating factor when studying music. As a matter of fact, *there is never a need to feel guilty about making or not making music.* If you choose not to practice one day, so be it. As you learn to recognize the connection between your practice time and your musical and technical growth, you can choose the pace at which you want to grow. Your teacher can help support you in these choices. He will also be able to guide you physically in the playing of your instrument, which can greatly affect the quality of the sounds you produce.

ADEQUATE PRACTICE TIME

A reasonable amount of practice time is the amount that you can comfortably fit into your day. In order to feel some growth and success, use five twenty-minute sessions each week as a minimum guideline. The frequency of your practice time is as important as, if not more important than, the amount of time you spend with your instrument at one sitting. Two hours on the weekend will not be nearly as beneficial as shorter periods scattered throughout the week.

If you really can practice for only twenty minutes a day, make sure that you are actually playing during that time. If you need to assemble or tune your instrument, do it before your twenty minutes begins. This can add an extra five or ten minutes, but it's important. It will be extremely difficult to make progress unless you're spending at least twenty minutes of actual playing time on your instrument.

As you develop your repertoire and feel the growth that comes with practice, you may find yourself at your instrument for increasingly longer periods of time without realizing it. When you are absorbed in a creative task, time tends to fly. Most often it is the approach to practicing that is the most difficult. As one music teacher told us, "The hardest thing about practicing the violin is opening the case!" Once at your instrument, you can begin to enjoy the musical involvement and your creative expressions.

When learning new music, one rule always applies: *The fastest way to progress is by going slowly.* This is often hard for new students to accept, and may seem paradoxical. It is, however, in keeping with what has been discovered about the operating characteristics of the brain and the neuromuscular system. The brain assimilates information in such a way that once a musical pattern is learned after slow, consistent practice, it can physically be played almost automatically while the musician concentrates on aesthetic performance.[5] If you already play an instrument, you may have experienced the ability to play a piece without much conscious thought as to where the next note is or where your hand should be. It is as if the piece technically plays itself. It is believed that once a pattern is learned by the brain through slow practice, the cerebellum—the part of the brain that helps regulate smoothness and timing of muscle contractions—takes over. At this point something "clicks," and musical passages can be played almost effortlessly.[6] Once you reach this level of physical integration, you can concentrate on dynamics, expression, articulation, and the full artistry of music-making.

So remember, practicing slowly *always* pays. Instead of focusing on the tempo, try to make slow practice as interesting as possible. Listen carefully to the tones you produce and to harmonies that may be highlighted with the added space and time. Be aware of the movement of your fingers as they strengthen and seem to take over by themselves. Think of slow practice as a type of meditation, rather than as a tedious activity. Hear each of the tones and how they move, connect, combine, and resolve.

Slow practicing will not always be fun or interesting. However, it will always result in your technical and musical growth. The more slow practice you do when learning new material, the faster you will be playing the pieces you love, and the sooner you will experience the emotional and physical benefits of playing your instrument.

Some ways to make practice time productive and enjoyable are by playing both old and new music during each session, sight-reading different pieces, and, if your repertoire is primarily classical, treating yourself every once in a while to playing a hit song you particularly enjoy or a jazz tune. Vary your repertoire. You have many moods and many emotions, and your musical repertoire can reflect them. By learning music with a variety of rhythms, melodies, and harmonies, you can match your mood, create a satisfying musical/emotional environment, and use the music to release tension, relax, or energize you.

Try to end your practice sessions on a satisfying note. Finish with a piece you play well or one you like a lot. Every now and then you may want to wrap up the session by listening to a special piece of instrumental music.

Practice sessions are times to be valued and respected. If you know that your practice time is between nine and ten at night, make sure that your friends know not to call you during that hour. Try to finish any pressing business before you sit down to play, so that you can be fully present in the music. Each time you practice, you give yourself a musical gift. At the end of the session, you will have mastered something new and grown as a musician and as a person.

OPPORTUNITIES TO SHARE MUSIC

Successful music-making involves a concept that many people find terrifying. For this reason, we've substituted the word *share* for *perform* in the fourth component of our program. Many people associate "performance" with expectation, criticism, and failure. Because of this, they don't consider how fulfilling it can be to play for others when the expectation and criticism aren't present.

Playing music for people who are nurturing and supportive can deeply satisfy the need to be listened to and heard, which we described in Chapter 1. Think of the way you feel when some-one listens attentively while you speak. This feeling can be height-ened immeasureably when it is your music to which that person is listening.

In Chapters 7 and 10, you learned a few ways to set up a

positive environment for playing music for others. Whether you play for one person or for one hundred, by sharing your music you can greatly enhance your sense of joy and success as a music-maker.

ACCEPTANCE OF UPS AND DOWNS

The ideal is to hold on to the belief that although time is often very limited, and interest tends to wane when one is out of touch with the instrument, it is worth continuing to study. Lessons can still be enjoyable even when practice time is at a minimum. The most important thing to remember is that letting time go by without playing is a choice. You can choose to reinvest your time and energy in your music again, just as you chose to let it go for a while. *You* are in control of how much enjoyment you can get out of your instrument.

Many beginners who start out learning an instrument with tremendous enthusiasm unfortunately do not learn how to sustain their interest and give up. Elizabeth Wolff, a pianist who has been performing and teaching for fifteen years, outlines four stages that beginning pianists can go through:

Exuberance: This stage usually lasts up to three months. During this time, the student buys all of the books, practices "like an angel," and delights in his progress.

Plateau: In this stage, difficulty with sight-reading usually begins to interfere with technical and musical progress. The student will begin to dwell on old music instead of moving ahead.

Bottoming-out: At this stage, the student feels that he "just can't do it": His hands don't work, he can't practice, and memorizing is an impossibility. Feelings of inadequacy are pervasive.

Rationalization: This stage is a feeble attempt at making sense of what has happened. The student claims that he didn't have time to practice at all. Guilt is rampant, and he feels that he has let himself down and didn't follow through on a discipline.

According to Wolff, there is a remedy for the decline in enthusiasm. First of all, the teacher must be supportive as the student discovers that making music is not all play and no work. There *is* work involved, and this work can be hard. It can also be challeng-

There are practical as well as social advantages and disadvan-
ges associated with different instruments. Although you will prob-
ly make your choice based upon your attraction to the sound
 a particular instrument, here is some additional information
at may be of help to you in making your decision:

E PIANO

The piano has always been one of the most popular instruments
cause it affords a wide range of expressive qualities. As opposed
 brass, wind, and string instruments, which mostly play melodic
es, the piano produces melody, rhythm, and harmony within
 ull spectrum of dynamics.

dvantages:

The piano is easy to learn, as demonstrated by the number
of children who take lessons each year.

A pianist receives excellent musical training, owing to many
experiences with harmony, melody, rhythm, dynamics, and their
integration.

As it is such a popular instrument, it is usually easy to find a
teacher.

The size of the piano can lend a feeling of power and strength
to the pianist.

Piano-playing utilizes a familiar, comfortable, and natural body
posture.

advantages:

Good pianos are expensive.

Except for electric keyboards, pianos are not portable. This
can be socially limiting, unless your musical friends agree to
come to your house.

Sight-reading piano music can be more difficult than reading
music for other instruments. One is presented with new perceptual challenges, since the reading is done both horizontally and
vertically at the same time.

Because of its size and dynamic range, some find playing the
piano a little overwhelming at first. It may take time to feel
comfortable at such a large instrument.

ing and enjoyable. In addition, the payoff is fantastic. If you find
yourself going through the last three stages, Wolff recommends
that first you catch yourself at the "plateau" stage and then:

- Approach the music in small blocks so that you don't feel
  overwhelmed. Work to master one unit at a time.
- Give yourself permission to regress for a while. Let yourself
  spend a week playing old, familiar music. This will help build
  your confidence and help you remember what the positive
  results of practicing have been and can be.
- Play what you know for a small, supportive audience.
- Sight-read music you love. The familiarity of music you've
  heard and enjoyed will help you have a more successful reading experience.
- Cut back on the amount of music you're learning.
- Give yourself permission to go through a slump. *No guilt!*
- Do anything that will help keep your motivation going. Attend
  a concert or buy yourself a new record. Remember that you
  are an active musician when you are listening to music as
  well as when you are playing your instrument.
- Keep your instrument in sight. If your instrument is the piano,
  this will not be difficult. If it is the flute or violin, however,
  there may be a tendency to move it out of the way when
  it's not in active use. No matter how much you are actually
  playing, always keep your instrument in view.
- Keep your music out, ready to be played. Let it be a reminder
  of the richness available to you through making music.[7]

• How to Choose the Right Instrument for You

Those people who have always had a musical dream may already
know which instrument they would like to play. Many persons,
however, wish to make music but don't know with what to start.
The choice of instrument is personal, and crucial for successful
music-making experiences. Your instrument is an extension of
yourself, a friend that can help you get to know your inner feelings
and communicate who you are to the world around you.

No one can tell you which instrument would be best for you.

A few studies have indicated that certain traits may be more prevalent among some groups of musicians than among others, but
these studies involved only small samples of musicians and therefore cannot be viewed as proof. One such study, recently completed
in England, supported previous findings that the trait of introver-
sion was common among string and woodwind players, while
extroversion was more common among brass musicians. The
woodwind players questioned seemed to have traits of shyness
and self-sufficiency. Aloofness, detachment, and critical awareness
were traits found in string players.[8]

Although the results of these studies are interesting, they are
not, as stated above, conclusive. There may be many extroverted
clarinetists and shy trombone players. You can use this information,
however, by considering the expressive capabilities of the different
instruments and evaluating which one may be best suited to your
personality. If you are a very vocal and vibrant person, an instrument with a pronounced quality and sound may be the right vehicle
for you. If, on the other hand, you are quiet or more private, an
instrument with a muted sound may be a better alternative.

Sometimes the most verbally understated person will choose
to play the drums, trumpet, or tuba. This is not unusual, and
can happen because of an imbalance in the meeting of their expressive needs. When someone won't express his opinions vocally
and yet feels permission to express fully on an instrument, he
may have come from a family of musicians, where children can
learn that in order to satisfy their needs for expression they must
do so through the music. In other cases, an individual may experience joy and exhilaration through music and determine on his
own that it is safe to release in music what is scary to express
in words. Thus, music-making can serve to meet expressive needs
when other outlets fail.

If you played an instrument as a child, you may or may not
have been able to choose which one it was. Often parents who
want their children to play make instrument choices for them
based on practical considerations, which don't allow for aesthetic
and emotional preference. According to Dr. Peter Ostwald, each
instrument holds a certain magic for a child:

> When a youngster is given music lessons, the shape, size,
> sound, and psychic meanings of the instrument may deeply

affect the nature of his thinking about hims
large. The piano, for instance, is a large, station
bling a piece of furniture which a child tends
his house, his parents, and other relatively pe
in the environment. Unlike a baby or a pet, th
kick, bite, or scream when it is poked. A piano ca
or pushed over and it is sturdy enough to with
violent assaults. With the piano one can perform
cal works without assistance of other instrum
permits solitude.

A young violinist has other advantages. H
small and he can embrace it like a doll, learnir
some of the real and imagined threats of beir
helpless child. The violin is fragile, and while
cannot play with it, he can clean his fiddle an
each day, or take it along for walks to school
of friends . . . the violinist needs others to play
ment drives him into orchestras . . . making
social creature compared to the solitary pianist

It is easy to see the psychological effects of pl
musical instruments.[9]

It is equally important for you as an adult to take
and social needs into account when choosing an insti
you prefer to play one that you can hug closely w
like a cello, or the piano, which stands on its own? I
making appeals to you, the guitar may be the instru
The best way to decide which instrument would
learning about the various instruments, listening to
at them, sensing which one you're drawn to, and
it will satisfy you musically, emotionally, and sociall

One wonderful way to learn more about the s
different instruments is by attending concerts. Watch
as they play, and listen to the individual sounds of the
Is there one sound that is particularly pleasing to
don't know which sound belongs to which instru
closely until you can connect the musician's actions wit
you hear. Imagine yourself playing that instrument.
imagine feeling as you play?

When at home, you can listen to recordings of pieces
instruments either on the radio or from your own c
you listen, feel which sounds attract and move you.

THE GUITAR

The guitar is another extremely popular instrument, owing to its pleasant sound, its portability, and the warmth it can lend to social gatherings. Like the piano, it is capable of producing rhythm, melody, and harmony, although in a more limited dynamic range (except when amplified). Different types of guitars are available for playing different styles of music. The most popular are the folk, classical, and electric.

Advantages:

1. The guitar can be taken anywhere.
2. It is quite easy to learn. With the knowledge of three chords, one can play much of the basic folk literature and enjoy being the music-maker at social get-togethers. The presence of a guitar is often an encouragement for others to sing, and to communicate with one another through music.
3. Guitars are available for a wide range of prices and can be relatively inexpensive. A good first instrument can be bought for as little as $100.
4. It is the easiest string instrument to tune.

Disadvantages:

1. Unless nylon strings are used to start, playing on steel strings, which have a more pronounced sound that many prefer, can result in fingertip blisters. Eventually calluses develop, which enable guitarists to play for long periods of time with no discomfort at all. Nylon strings are often a better choice for beginners.
2. Tuning can be a problem at the beginning for those who have difficulty matching pitches.

STRING INSTRUMENTS

The string instruments, which include primarily the violin, viola, cello, and double bass, can be found in country, rock, jazz, and folk groups as well as in orchestras. The guitar and the harp are also technically members of this group.

Advantages:

1. Learning a string instrument can promote the development of musical skills. The instrument demands the discrimination

of fine subtleties in pitch and timbre. Since there are no frets
or indications of where to place the fingers on the fingerboard,
the musical ear is forced to develop in order to produce the
desired sound. Tuning the instrument also helps the development of these skills.

2. As one violinist who plays for the New York Metropolitan Opera
   told us, "How you move is the sound you get." Because of
   the unique connection between the quality of body movement
   and the quality of sound produced, the playing of a string
   instrument can aid in the development of body awareness.

3. String instruments, especially the violin and viola, are portable.

4. As a string player, you will be welcome in many different types
   of ensembles, and can enjoy the benefits of musical communication with others.

Disadvantages:

1. There are fewer visual cues on the string instruments than on
   any of the other instruments, which can be difficult for a beginner. As stated above, however, this eventually leads to the development of more fine-tuned musical skills.

2. String instruments are more difficult to tune than other instruments.

3. They can be extremely expensive. For this reason, rentals are
   popular for beginning students.

4. Playing a string instrument requires a different type of coordination than many people are used to, since one hand uses the
   bow, and the other is responsible for fingering. This coordination comes with practice.

5. Some teachers claim that the violin and the viola can be unusu-
   ally tiring to play, since they must be held up for a period of
   time. With proper training, however, one can learn quickly how
   to move with the instrument so as to avoid this problem.

6. Some string players may develop calluses on their fingers, depending upon how they play their instruments.

7. Many teachers agree that because of the musical and physical
   coordination involved, learning a string instrument usually requires more practice time than the minimum twenty minutes
   mentioned earlier in this chapter.

WOODWIND INSTRUMENTS

Woodwind instruments can be found in every type of musical ensemble. While the most popular are the flute, clarinet, recorder, and saxophone, this instrument category also includes the piccolo, alto flute, oboe, bass clarinet, E-flat clarinet (there are a few other clarinets as well), bassoon, and English horn.

Advantages:

1. All of the woodwinds are easily portable.
2. The popular woodwind instruments are relatively inexpensive. Recorders can be bought for as little as $10, while flutes, clarinets, and saxophones for beginners range from approximately $150 to $250.
3. The flute, saxophone, oboe, recorder, and, to an extent, the clarinet work on the same basic fingering principle except for a few minor changes. For this reason, any piece learned on one instrument is transferable to another. This is why one person in a band is often seen playing a variety of woodwinds.
4. As a woodwind player, you can enjoy the benefits of ensemble playing.
5. The recorder can be learned extremely quickly, because it is easy to blow. The embouchure, or mouth position, for the clarinet is easier than that for the flute, but both can be learned within a few short weeks.
6. When playing a woodwind instrument, you can stretch your breathing capacity to its limit. This can result in some of the benefits of aerobic exercise, such as a relaxed body and a lower pulse rate. One clarinetist we interviewed claims that his at-rest pulse rate of 45 is a combined result of his running and his playing. His doctor agrees.

Disadvantages:

1. Many woodwinds use reeds to produce sound, which must be changed every two or three weeks. These are inexpensive, however, and are easy to change once one is taught how.
2. Some say that certain dental conditions, such as missing teeth, can be a problem when playing a woodwind instrument. This

is not necessarily true for everyone with this condition. If you are determined to play, you'll be able to play.

3. As woodwind instruments play only melodic lines, ensemble playing is necessary for a harmonic experience.

BRASS INSTRUMENTS

The most popular brass instruments are the trumpet, trombone, French horn, and tuba. There are many others to choose from, although they don't receive as much exposure as those just mentioned. They are the cornet, flügelhorn, valve trombone, euphonium, baritone horn, mellophone, E-flat alto horn, bass trombone, and sousaphone. The brass are melodic instruments and can be found in any type of musical ensemble, including rock bands, jazz bands, orchestras, and chamber groups.

Advantages:

1. While all brass instruments are portable, the trumpet and smaller brass are especially easy to carry around.
2. Learning to play a brass instrument can be of particular assistance in the development of the musical ear. Brass players learn how to distinguish pitches in a way that is different from that of other instrumentalists.
3. Because of the wide variety of dynamic range, brass instruments can help you express a wide variety of emotions. They are capable of producing extremely loud sounds, as well as sounds that are soft and sensitive.
4. All of the valve instruments, which include all brass instruments except the trombone, have the exact same fingerings. Although most brass players choose to play only one instrument (as opposed to woodwind players, who are encouraged to "double" on other woodwinds), this knowledge would make it easier to learn another brass instrument if desired.
5. The popular brass instruments are not very expensive. As long as an excellent mouthpiece is used, an excellent sound can be produced on a $150 student instrument. Mouthpieces are extremely inexpensive but make a tremendous difference in the sound produced.
6. A brass player's sounds are always heard!

Disadvantages:

1. The first week of playing can be difficult and discouraging for the beginner. All kinds of strange, funny, and embarrassing sounds will emerge as the student struggles to control muscles he has never paid attention to before.
2. As is true of others who play melodic instruments, brass players do not have harmonic experiences unless they make music with others.
3. The brass instruments may be disturbing to roommates and/or neighbors, owing to the loud sounds produced. You will need to work out a practice schedule with this in mind.

PERCUSSION INSTRUMENTS

The term *percussion* comprises a wide range of instruments, only some of which are listed below. They include orchestral percussion—tympani, marimbas, xylophone, and the varied bells and gongs used for special effects; jazz percussion—vibraphone, rock percussion (which includes the drum, or "trap," set); Latin percussion—conga drums, bongos, maracas; and ethnic percussion—everything from African drums to Chinese temple blocks. While many of the instruments require considerable skill and training, some, such as the bongos and the tambourine, can be played successfully by anyone.

Advantages:

1. Rock percussion can be relatively inexpensive, and Latin percussion can be extremely inexpensive. A used drum set can be bought for $150, while bongos may cost as little as $25.
2. Once you learn a few rhythm patterns, you can play a percussion instrument along with hundreds of tunes.
3. The drums are extremely popular because of our natural attraction to and need for rhythm. Playing the drums can satisfy the need to hear and express rhythm in an enjoyable manner.
4. Smaller percussion, such as the tambourine, conga, or bongos, can be played in a park, on the beach, or at a party. They are easily portable.
5. Most musical groups need a percussionist. The opportunities for playing with others are plentiful.

Disadvantages:

1. Drum sets are difficult to transport, and take up more space than many of the other instruments.
2. As percussion instruments are mostly rhythmic in nature, percussionists do not enjoy harmonic experiences unless they play with others or along with recordings.
3. As with the brass instruments, the volume of many percussion instruments can be irritating to family, friends, and especially neighbors. You may need to arrange your practice time with their schedules in mind.

There are hundreds of instruments that do not fall into the categories described here but that many people enjoy playing. Included in this list would be the accordion, harmonica, dulcimer, bagpipes, kazoo, spoons, washboard, kalimba, and ukelele. Some of these originate from ethnic cultures. Others, such as the spoons and washboard, became musical instruments when "real" ones were not available and the need to make rhythmic music was strong. You actually have a complete jug band in your kitchen at this very moment! Your assortment of pots are metal drums, while their lids are crash cymbals. Drinking glasses become melodious when struck lightly, and can produce popular tunes when filled with varied amounts of liquid. Wooden or metal utensils make great drum or rhythm sticks. In addition, your voice can add to this "joyful noise" as you sing along with the music.

There are times when even the most timid person needs to make music. If you don't yet own the instrument of your dreams, you still can make music and love it, as described in the following story:

On a sunny afternoon downtown on Constitution Plaza, Skip LaPlante set out his instruments—dented pots and pans, rusted iron pipes, scraps of sheet metal—and invited passersby to help make music.

About 50 people joined in. But the star was Frances Danforth. She leaned forward in her wheelchair, swaying to and fro, banging a tin can with a stick in time to the conga-like beat. Mrs. Danforth is 81 years old.

"What's a nice girl like me doing in a place like this?" she shouted, still whacking the can. "You've got to be yourself. You've got to let your hair down. You've got to go with the flow. Just look at the rhythm and the energy. Loosen up."[10]

If you have ever wanted to play an instrument and never believed you could, don't wait any longer to begin. Choose to join the world of fulfilled music-makers. Let music do for you what it has done for millions. Find a way to make music, and let yourself in on the pleasure, growth, and internal peace that can be the result.

12

Singing Your Heart Out

Within you lies the most magical musical instrument of all. The human voice conveys who we are through a unique combination of rhythm, melody, timbre, and dynamics. Just as there is no one with the same face as yours, there is no voice like your own. It is a personal vehicle for expression of yourself.

Since infancy, your voice has been a primary means of self-expression. The melodious sounds you emitted as an infant and toddler were your expressions of sheer joy and wonder at discovering the world around you. Singing was an effortless, acceptable means of being yourself.

Now, throughout the day, your voice communicates the meanings of your words through rhythm, melody, and dynamics. It is obvious that the phrase "I am fine" can be communicated truthfully, angrily, sarcastically, warmly, or humorously, depending upon the tonal inflections and volume of your voice. When a close friend or relative calls, you can usually tell when something is wrong by the sound of his voice. Similarly, when a person feels vibrant, energized, and positive, his voice will usually reflect this in its resonant, melodious, musical sound.

Singing involves the full use of the voice and of the self. As the ultimate musical instrument, the voice is unsurpassed as an expressive medium. While singing, we do not express *through* an instrument; we *become* the instrument. The vibrations created by singing can bring your body, mind, and spirit to life.

Singing is a common sign of joy. Many of us sing or hum to ourselves when feeling content or excited. While walking down Fifth Avenue a few years ago, we were surprised to find a well-dressed businessman walking energetically next to us singing "Oh,

What a Beautiful Morning!" in a full, loud voice. At one point he stopped and explained, "I just got a new job!" As he burst into song, he allowed himself to express his joy and pride over his accomplishment. As evident from such songs as "Whistle While You Work," "Singin' in the Rain," "I Want to Teach the World to Sing," and countless others, singing and pleasurable feelings have been known to go hand in hand.

In his book *The Voice of Neurosis,* Dr. Paul Moses, who has studied and written in depth of the connection between the voice and personality, discusses the stage of infancy when singing develops. At around six months, the baby begins repeating syllables for the kinesthetic pleasure involved. "Lalling," as vocalization is called at this stage, satisfies oral needs and surrounds the child with his own rhythms and sounds. According to Moses, there may be a connection between this stage and our feelings about singing in general: "Perhaps it is because voice production in this wordless age leaves solely agreeable memories that we have the urge later in life to sing when we are happy and gay."[1] Singing can also be a way to change your negative frame of mind to a positive one. You will learn how to do this further along in this chapter.

Singing is for everyone. Yet, even though we are born with the natural ability to sing, enjoy doing so in our youth, and are attracted to music throughout our lives, it is amazing how many people learn to associate fear and anxiety with this enjoyable act. The reasons why this occurs often begin with an uncomfortable singing environment, rather than with the singing experience itself.

For example, when you were in elementary school, you probably had group-singing experiences in your classroom or in an assembly. If your teacher was supportive and competent, he would have focused on the enjoyment involved in singing, while gently directing those who had difficulty singing in tune or projecting their voices. Chances are, however, that those children who needed extra coaching didn't receive it but were either admonished or humiliated. The two most common stories we hear are of those people who were told to mouth the words during singing, and those who were told to sit in the back of the room until they could sing in tune. For these children, the chances of ever singing in front of others become practically nonexistent. The memories of these experiences remain vivid for the rest of their lives.

If you have had either of the experiences mentioned above and wish that you could sing, it is time to leave those memories in the past, where they belong. It is never too late to begin to sing, even if your voice sounds unpleasant to you at this moment.

Just as there are myths that serve to keep us from experiencing the joys of playing an instrument, there are myths that serve to inhibit us from using our voices. The most prevalent of these are:

1. "I can't carry a tune."
2. "I'll always be too embarrassed to sing in front of others."
3. "I'll never be able to sing really well."
4. "Singing is just a form of entertainment. It can't really *do* anything for me."

Rather than believing these myths, you can begin to expand your physical, emotional, intellectual, and spiritual experiences by opening yourself to song.

Myth 1: "I can't carry a tune."

Many people claim that they can't carry a tune, so they don't sing. These persons can often remember incidents of family members telling them to be quiet or covering their ears when they began to open their mouths. Singing out of tune is most often due to a lack of experience in listening closely to music. One singing teacher we know teaches students to sing in tune within one lesson, by helping them to listen closely to and imitate both her speaking and singing voice.

If you don't sing in tune, it is still possible for you to learn. The only limitation on your learning to produce sounds that are in tune would be an actual hearing or vocal impairment. There are even persons with these difficulties who have learned to match pitches. You don't have to continue believing that you have "two left ears." It's never too late to get the encouragement and training you missed as a child.

Myth 2: "I'll always be too embarrassed to sing in front of others."

Singing is expressive of the self, and those who are uncomfortable with themselves will often avoid singing. Many people will not sing in front of others, which accounts for the shower stall's being the most popular singing environment. Recently published was a plastic shower songbook designed to expand our shower repertoire!

While singing in the shower is a fun, self-affirming, and satisfying release, singing in other surroundings can be even more fulfilling. The embarrassment you may feel when letting others hear your voice will diminish with experience. You will feel more comfortable as you become familiar with your voice and learn to appreciate its unique qualities. Let the exercises in this chapter help you give yourself permission to release your voice, so that you can begin to feel the joys and benefits of sharing songs with those around you.

As singing becomes more a part of your daily routine, you may even consider joining a community ensemble or chorus. Of the singers with whom we spoke, nearly twice as many claimed that they preferred singing with others to singing alone, and over ninety percent claimed to experience social benefits as a direct result of singing with others—a sense of enjoyment, a sense of shared communication, a sense of belonging, a way to spend time with others, a sense of purpose, and a sense of personal recognition.

Group singing can be found in practically every culture as a means of sharing joy, grief, love, and unity. It is a means of hearing your own unique sound blending with those around you. In this sense, singing in a group is a metaphor for life itself. Your own voice is heard, and your sense of self is expressed. In addition, you have a place in the community that supports you and that helps you fulfill your expressive needs. Sometimes you sing out, and sometimes you silently listen to others as they sing in turn. The group-singing experience represents the balance and blend of the individual and the community.

Singing in a group is a wonderful way to meet people. In addition, you may be able to participate in some special musical experiences. Community choruses are often asked to sing with orchestras for pieces that call for large numbers of voices. When these situations arise, you may be afforded the opportunity to sing under the direction of different conductors, sing with live orchestral accompaniment, meet other musicians, and participate in gala concert events. These can be thrilling musical and emotional experiences that you may never forget. The overwhelmingly joyous feelings that singing in a group can elicit frequently trigger peak experiences, which, as discussed in Chapter 7, can positively influence your feelings about yourself and your life.

Myth 3: "I'll never be able to sing really well."

In the singing exercises outlined in Chapters 6 through 10, there were no directions given on how to sing "correctly," or as fully as possible. We showed you how to experience your voice creatively and how to communicate more effectively with your voice with another person. Singing, no matter how you do it, is an enjoyable experience. When singing at a campfire or in a car with friends, let your voice flow naturally. Remember that no matter what you may have heard about your voice in the past, you have the *right* to sing. By singing more often, and listening carefully to the voices around you, you can begin to hear how your voice fits in and tune it to others. This process often occurs naturally once a person lets go of past memories and becomes involved in music-making.

You can change your use of your voice. When you were little, you probably heard many things from others about yourself that you have already changed. Were there subjects that were difficult for you in which you now excel? Were you referred to as shy, whereas now you speak your mind without hesitation? In the same vein, an evaluation of your vocal abilities handed down by a one-time authority figure does not have to be accepted for life, unless you let it. You can change your voice itself and you can change your feelings about your voice. Because the sound of your voice is reflective of your inner life, by altering the use of your voice you can change your feelings about yourself as a whole. As Alexander Lowen, creator of Bioenergetics, states, "a rich voice is a rich manner of self-expression, and denotes a rich inner life."[2]

To begin to feel the benefits of singing, all you need do is think of a song, open your mouth, and let out the sounds. On one hand, this can be thought of as the simplest activity in the world. On the other hand, in order to reap the full benefits that singing can bring, it is essential that you learn how to breathe fully, align your body correctly, and begin with an expansive, positive frame of mind. You will immediately hear the difference in the sounds you create. Further, you will experience ongoing benefits, such as heightened emotions, improved speaking voice, better posture, and a more confident sense of self.

Anyone can learn how to sing fully. In order to do so, however, it is necessary that you have a good teacher. The exercises given throughout this chapter should be viewed only as a way to get started breathing, standing, and thinking in a way that is conducive to sounding your best. Also, these exercises are not devised purely for singing. Good singing is the result of the body and mind at their best. Therefore, these exercises can be viewed as ways to prepare for any full use of the self.

Myth 4: "Singing is just a form of entertainment. It can't really *do* anything for me."

Aside from the benefits already mentioned, singing can help you breathe more deeply, improve your posture, bring you emotional awareness and fulfillment, and enhance your speaking voice. In addition, relaxation is very often a by-product of singing well. One professional singer who took her first singing lesson in her twenties relates the following story:

> When I decided to take voice lessons, I assumed that I would first have to learn how to relax. I was a very tense person, and imagined having to do relaxation exercises before I could produce a pleasant sound. What actually happened, to my surprise, was the exact opposite. My teacher had me start singing right away, and by learning to sing correctly, I became fully relaxed. This was an incredible revelation to me! Even now, the more I sing, the more I even *think* about singing, the more relaxed I can get.

This is not an unusual story. And it illustrates why choruses are sought out by amateur singers. Most choruses hold rehearsals on weeknights, yet are filled with professionals who work long hours. Singing provides a release from the day's tensions and, through deep, full breathing, enables the singer to feel centered and grounded after a hard day's work.

The deep breathing that occurs when one sings fully is responsible for much of the relaxing effect. In addition, the tones produced can have both an energizing and a calming effect on the body. Lisa Sokolov, a certified music therapist working in New York

City, uses this principle in her work: "Tone is a physical phenomenon that sets matter into motion. By creating tone, a person can activate and release the physical body."[3] The musical practices of many of the Eastern religions demonstrate the belief that certain tones affect certain areas of the body and, when played or sung, can release tensions in these areas. While there is no evidence to support this theory, it is important to note that many persons have been emotionally enriched, spiritually uplifted, and physically healed as a result of these practices.

Certain ways of using the voice have been described as resulting in particular spiritual and physical benefits. Toning, an ancient healing method that was studied and written about by Laurel Elizabeth Keyes, is the release of the physical body through sound. This happens naturally when we yawn, grunt as we lift heavy objects, or groan during childbirth. Toning can be practiced daily for numerous benefits. When she first began practicing "Toning," Keyes wrote:

> As I continued to experiment with this body-voice I realized that there was much more to it than just a release of tension. Each time that I Toned, my body felt exhilarated, alive as it had never felt before; a feeling of wholeness and extreme well being. . . . When I let [the Tone] pass out, freely, with no attempt to control it, it appeared to cleanse the entire body, releasing tensions and congested areas. . . . I was convinced that there had to be a relationship between this natural body-voice and the mind without conflict, and with benefit to both.[4]

Other writers, such as Rudolf Steiner, Sufi Inayat Khan, and Ravi Shankar, write of the positive spiritual results of producing sound with the voice. According to their theories and the beliefs prevalent within Eastern religious sects, singing is a means of grounding and centering the self, of attaining spiritual heights, and of opening the entire realm of spiritual and emotional wealth to the self.

Singing is also a way to change how you are feeling. Over eighty-five percent of the singers we surveyed said that they used singing to change their mood. Catherine Roe, a professional singer and teacher of voice at Sarah Lawrence College, shared with us that when she feels particularly sad, she can change her mood through singing. She begins with songs that reflect her sadness, singing them softly while accompanying herself on the autoharp or piano. As she gives expression to her sadness, she releases it, and then begins to sing more uplifting songs. By the end of an hour, she sings songs that are expressive of a positive frame of mind.

The reason that it is possible to change your mood through singing may be the same reason given for being able to change your mood through listening. Feelings by nature are dynamic, not static. They exist and change according to a person's emotional, physical, biological, mental, and social environment. Music is a dynamic medium as well, and when music matches a given mood through its rhythms, melodies, and harmonies, emotions can be expressed and released. The iso-moodic principle, which refers to music listening, maintains that a person's mood can be altered by listening first to music that matches the existing mood and then to pieces that gradually change in the direction of the desired mood.[5] In Chapter 15, you will learn how to evaluate the music that is reflective of your moods and use it in this manner. The same can be true of singing, as described in Roe's experience. Try it yourself when in a private place, or among others who share a particular feeling with you.

While there are countless positive benefits of singing, one that particularly stands out is the intimacy afforded through vocal exchange. Singing to someone can be one of the most emotional ways of communicating your feelings. This stems from the pure, wordless communication that takes place between mother and infant. Singing is one of the means by which mothers and infants establish their unique relationship. It is through vocal exchange that feelings, sensations, and a sense of contentment are expressed and shared. At this point, singing can come to represent the experience of intimacy and satisfaction. Later on in life, whether singing a hit song with a classmate, a romantic song to a loved one, or a lullabye to your own child or grandchild, you can experience a heightened sense of intimacy as a result of this connection.

If you have kept yourself from singing for whatever reason, you have kept yourself from experiencing one of the most natural sources of fulfillment available to you. You already have the instrument necessary, and while it may be a little rusty from lack of use, you can be guaranteed that it still works. You have the right to sing no matter what you think your voice sounds like. Here are some points to remember to help you get started.

1. *Enjoy your private moments in song.* Whether in the shower or alone in the house, let your voice go. Sing along with the music you hear whether it comes from the radio, the stereo, or inside yourself.

2. *Give yourself permission to sing in a group.* This may be in church or synagogue, at a campfire, at a party, or at a ball game. Also, explore your options for joining a community singing group. If you truly want to sing with others, you can find a way to do so.

3. *If you have a baby or a young child, sing to and with him.* By doing so, you will provide him with emotional as well as aesthetic fulfillment and both of you will benefit from the shared intimacy and beauty of the moment.

• The Hows and Whys of Singing Your Best

It is precisely the actions that are the cause of full singing that are also its results. When you sing correctly, a cycle of growth is created. By fully expanding the body and breathing correctly, by developing good posture, and by beginning with a positive frame of mind, you will produce tones that are pleasing to the ear and expressive. As a result of the aesthetic, emotional, and physical pleasure that full singing brings, you can be motivated to incorporate these actions into your daily repertoire of expression.

BREATHING

One of the most potent causes and results of singing is the fuller use of breath. While you are singing, the increased expansion of the diaphragmatic muscles causes air to rush in and fill your lungs, and you feel the effects of deep breathing. Many experience this sensation to be relaxing at the same time it is energizing.

Breath and life have always been connected. Beginning with the Bible, which tells how God breathed life into Adam, we can begin to understand that breath does more than sustain us physically. For thousands of years the Hindus and Zen Buddhists have preached the importance of full, deep breathing for a richer physi-

cal, emotional, and spiritual life. Through Yogic breathing practices, students are instructed how to rid the body of toxins through
exhalation, and renew the body's energy with new breath through
inhalation. These practices continue to be taught and studied
throughout the world today.

Wilhelm Reich was among the first in the Western world to
draw a connection between the breath and the emotions. According
to his theories and to those of his students, while full breathing
allows for full feeling, shallow breathing can reflect the cutting
off of one's emotions and the natural flow of life energy in the
body.[6] Picture your reaction when something shocking or scary
happens to you. Most often you will automatically hold your breath
and put your feelings on "hold" for a moment. Once the shock
is over and you resume breathing, you may feel the emotional
effects of the incident begin to "hit." Many of us may breathe in
a shallow manner much of the time as a means of protecting
ourselves from feelings we wish not to experience. We do this
unconsciously.

Therapists who realize the connection between breath and the
emotions ask their clients to become aware of their breathing as
they speak. With this awareness, the client can begin to breathe
fully and experience the feelings that accompany the content of
his words. In the experiencing of these feelings can come release,
understanding, and resolution of the issue.

According to Reich, repressed feelings can actually be stored
in areas of the physical body.[7] Through full breathing and awareness of these areas, the repressed feelings and memories, and
the tension that accompanies them, can be released.

Full singing involves full utilization of breath. With the combination of breathing and the music chosen, the singer can reach new
heights of feeling and expression. Continued full breathing can
actually become the result of the singing experience as well. Of
the singers we interviewed, ninety-eight percent claimed to experience emotional changes as a direct result of singing. While over
ninety percent mentioned having feelings of pleasure, most of
the singers we questioned also felt joy, peace, and exhilaration
while engaged in song.

Lisa Sokolov has done extensive work using the voice as a
healing tool for the body and the emotions. She works with breath
as a means of releasing what is stored in the body. According

to Sokolov: "Bringing breath to an area is like bringing illumination to an area. Singing, therefore, becomes an exploration of the self."[8] As a result of this work, a greater integration can take place among all aspects of the personality. Sokolov views the throat as a valve, which leads and opens to what exists underneath. When a person is releasing himself in song, the mental and emotional components of the self become connected. "The throat," she continues, "is a physical and symbolic bridge between the head and the heart. Therefore singing can become a way of developing a relationship between the mind and the emotions."[9]

It is for this reason that many persons crave singing while others are afraid of it. Those who spend their days in intellectual pursuit may feel the need for the aesthetic stimulation and emotional release that singing brings. Others, however, who feel more secure in the realm of intellect than with their emotions, may resist singing as a means of defending against their feelings.

It is precisely through singing that you can begin to feel and express more of your emotions. By doing so, you will experience a greater sense of your individuality and of your power.

To begin feeling the effects of full breathing and singing, think of breathing as a process of expanding the body. Inhalation is actually a result of muscle movement, not the cause of it. When your diaphragm and lungs expand, a vacuum is created within the lungs and an air mass moves in. When the muscles contract, air is expelled. So, instead of "taking a breath" while sticking the shoulders and chest up and out, throwing the body out of line, "let" yourself breathe by expanding the torso.

The easiest way to see and feel how your body breathes most naturally is to perform the following exercise:

Exercise 12-1

Lie down on the floor on your back. Place one hand on your chest and the other on your belly. See if you can get into the frame of mind for sleep. Feel your hands rise and fall as your body expands and contracts naturally while it takes in and releases air.

In order to feel the full expansion of your body as you continue lying on the floor, place your hands right above your waistline at your sides, enclosing the area between your thumb and the other fingers. Now push in forcibly against the diaphragm muscle as your body expands. Continue giving your body the resistance, and your ability to expand, maintain the expansion, and breathe fully will improve.

Try singing a tone or a familiar melody as you breathe in this position. Listen for the difference in your voice between the way you usually sound and the way you sound now. Let your voice express what you are feeling in the moment.

Working within these guidelines will help you develop your body expansion so that you have enough strength to sing long, full phrases. By continuing to do this, especially under the guidance of a teacher, you will be able to sing the songs you love with confidence and pride. You will develop a renewed, deepened sense of contact with yourself and with those with whom you share your songs.

POSTURE

Another positive result of full singing is improved posture. This is a result of singing, again, only because it is one of the causes. Without the establishment and maintenance of a correct body position, you may release tones that are out of tune and harsh to the ear. Poor posture can strain your body, and physical problems can result.

When you are singing in a right position, your body will feel dynamic, not static. There will be a flow of breath and energy through it, and a sense of strength to support the tones you release. Your body will come alive.

By singing correctly, you remind your body of the posture that it naturally craves. This sensation stays with you. During the day, whether at work or at home, you can revitalize your body as you did while singing by establishing good posture and maintaining it while you speak. This can serve to increase your confidence and sense of self-esteem.

As mentioned earlier, working with a singing teacher is the best way for you to learn how to sing fully and feel the results. A good teacher will help you align your body correctly, help you release rather than tighten as you produce sound, help you choose repertoire to your liking, and accompany you both musically and emotionally on your journey as a singer. If you cannot work with a teacher, here are some ways to get started using your body in such a way that you can enjoy the benefits of singing correctly.

The best way to align your body for singing and speaking is to pay attention to the spine:

Exercise 12-2

As you stand or sit, stretch the spine. Reach for the ceiling with the top of the spine and to the floor with the bottom. Let the crown of your head reach for the ceiling as well. It is often helpful to picture an imaginary string that goes from the ceiling through the top of the head, through the spine, and down to the floor. Imagine a hand gently pulling up the string. Release your shoulders and arms so that they can swing freely. Make sure that your knees are unlocked.

You will know that you are aligned incorrectly if your shoulders are rounded, your chest is caved in, flat, or jutting out, or if your abdomen or rear end is tightened or protruding.

Try sitting in a straight-backed chair so that you can focus on your spine alone. Let yourself feel the difference between your usual posture and this one. Breathe fully and gently without throwing your body out of line. As you breathe, feel the muscles in your abdomen and back expand. You may be able to feel your back push against the back of the chair.

From this position, try yawning and letting a sound emerge. Do this a few times, and feel the release. Then, while fully expanded, begin to sing a familiar tune. Try singing with "ah" or "la" at first. Listen to the quality of your voice. What does it feel like to hear yourself sing? When you feel ready, add words. Close your eyes, stay fully expanded, and release your voice.

FRAME OF MIND

You have just learned some of the technical points of full singing, which anyone can be taught to do. There are many other physical items to attend to, such as the jaw, the facial muscles, and the lower torso. Singing involves the whole body, and when done correctly, energizes the whole body.

Perhaps the main prerequisite for full singing is a positive frame of mind. With the release of your mind comes release of the strengths of your body. In turn, your mind can be affected by the act of singing. One teacher told us of students who enter his studio in a bad mood, and with activation of the muscles of the body, full breathing, proper alignment of the body, and full use of the voice, emerge from their lessons feeling positive and energetic. Many of the emotional benefits of singing have been discussed earlier in this chapter. Through involvement in the creative act of full singing, one can re-experience an expansive frame of both mind and body.

• Improving Your Speaking Voice Through Song

As the singing voice and speaking voice are essentially the same, through singing you can become more aware of the full expressive capabilities of your voice, and make use of them to enhance your presence when communicating with others.

Alexander Lowen regards the voice as a reflection of the personality: "A person who speaks in a monotone has a very limited range of expression, and we tend to equate this with a limited personality. A voice can be flat, without depth or resonance, it can be low as if lacking energy, and it can be thin and bodiless. Each of these qualities bears some relationship to the personality of the individual."[10] Picture someone you know whose voice is flat and expressionless. Is he basically expressionless in his behavior as well? Is he limited in the amount of life he expresses through his words and actions? Now think of your own voice. Is it as expressive as you would like it to be? Lowen continues: "If a person is to recover his full potential for self-expression, it is important he gain full use of his voice in all its registers and in all its nuances of feeling."[11]

Singing is intensified, prolonged speech. When used correctly, your voice becomes a dynamic, rich vehicle of sound and expression. It can be soft and caressing, as well as big and expansive. It can soar in the higher registers and boom in the bass. You can learn to let your voice be sexy, powerful, intense, and relaxed. Sometimes your speaking voice will automatically become more expressive and resonant as a result of singing. Very often, however, persons who sing conjure up the image and feeling of singing when they wish to express themselves in particular ways in speech.

Knowing how to use the range and volume of the voice can help you when you're giving a presentation, asking for a promotion, communicating something important to another person, or simply expressing yourself. With the help of the melodies of your voice, you can get across your message loud and clear. Your sense of confidence and self-esteem will be affected as you see how people respond to the new ways in which you present yourself.

Singing may also be particularly helpful to you if you have a speech problem. While production of the singing and speaking voice are the same, singing and speaking are actions that emanate from two different hemispheres of the brain. Speaking comes from the left hemisphere, singing from the right. Research has shown that it is because of this split that certain speech problems, such as stuttering, disappear while one is singing. Although singing may not cure the problem, someone who stutters can gain tremendous confidence through the free, uninterrupted flow of the voice which is afforded in song.

Whether you wish to learn to relax, improve your breathing, posture, or speaking voice, or just have fun, singing is one of the most accessible, affordable, and available means of doing so. Use the guidelines in this chapter to help you learn how to release your voice. Your voice, in all its forms, is a reflection of who you are. In addition to enjoying your sounds in private, let the world hear your song. Singing will help you express yourself more fully, help you develop a more confident sense of self, help you develop stronger and more intimate communications with others, and help you participate more actively in the harmony of life.

IV
Listening
to Music:
A Spectrum
of Sound

Music and rhythm find
their way into the secret
places of the soul.
—Plato

13

Listen to What You Hear

Music listening is the most available form of music participation there is. Anyone can listen to music, regardless of skill, age, talent, or health. Modern advances in the recording industry and electronics have made it possible to listen to music anytime and anywhere. Waterproof radios, portable cassette players, headsets, and car stereos have all contributed to the increasing accessibility of music listening. In addition, high technology now brings you the finest in recorded or transmitted sound ever. All you need do is open your ears.

Sales of records, radios, stereos, cassette tapes, and other music paraphernalia indicate that more people than ever are listening to music. The simplest explanation for this phenomenon is that music listening must be creating desirable effects, such as mental, physical, emotional, and spiritual well-being. Most of the time we listen to music for a reason, to cheer us up, slow us down, or enhance a feeling. If music did not create such desirable effects, there would be little explanation as to why we choose to listen to so much music so much of the time.

From our discussion in Chapter 5, you may already have discovered the ways, whens, and whys you use music in your life. In this chapter, we will explore what is known about the effects listening to music has upon your being. This will help you understand why you choose the music you listen to, and will add to your collection of ideas as to how to make music work for you.

• What We Know

That music can be used to bring about changes in mental, physical, emotional, and spiritual states has been known and written about since time immemorial. As early as 600 B.C., Thales is said to have cured a plague in Sparta by means of music. Many of us are familiar with the biblical story of King Saul, who called upon David to play the harp for him in order to soothe his fits of melancholia and anger. As it is written in the Bible:

> And it came to pass when the evil spirit from God was upon Saul, that David took up a harp and played with his hand; so that Saul was refreshed and was well and the evil spirit departed from him.[1]

This story clearly reveals King Saul's belief in the power of music upon his spirit and emotions, and indicates that he probably subscribed to the age-old adage "Music hath charms to soothe the savage breast." Thus, from the earliest records of our culture, proof exists that people have long believed in the powerful effects of music.

For some, the story of David and King Saul may be looked upon merely as dramatic legend or myth. Yet, we do not have to look far to know that music may profoundly affect our spiritual and emotional selves. Certainly we have all had the experience of being saddened by a slow and melancholy song, or suddenly uplifted by the upbeat sound of a marching band. Many of us allow our spirits to be touched each year when we hear religious music during holiday times.

It is easy to detect the immediate effects music often has on our bodies. This may be anything from that irresistible urge to tap your feet or sway to a perky rhythm, to the quickening of your heartbeat at the sound of a dramatic drum roll and cymbal crash. These are simple examples of the powerful effect that music may have on your body. On a deeper level, American Indians regularly incorporated music into their healing ceremonies, believing it to possess as much curative value as certain plants. Interestingly, plants were believed to be effective *only* when the right song or incantation was added. Today, music in modern hospitals and other health-care settings is becoming increasingly popular as the practice of music therapy becomes more well known and widespread. These modern practices of healing with music still draw upon the knowledge of the ancients, who viewed music as a potent source of emotional and physical health.

Our minds, too, are constantly affected by sound and music. To appreciate this fact, you need only think of the wealth of associations, imagery, thoughts, and ideas that are sparked by a single song. Indeed, your mental response certainly plays as important a role in your choices of and preferences for particular types of music as do your physical, spiritual, and emotional responses. Think of how often you have bought a piece of music or a record because it reminds you of a certain time, place, or person. Or, think of how many times you have turned to a special radio station because of the "state of mind" you are hoping the music they play will induce. In these instances, you are inviting and allowing music to have a particular effect on your mental state.

• Discovering the Effects of Music

In addition to all that we intuitively sense about the effects of music upon us, the search for scientific validation, along with the development of the field of music therapy, has provided a rich foundation of writing and research about music and its effects on the mind, body, spirit, and emotions. Almost all of this research is based on the responses of music listeners, as opposed to music players or singers. This makes sense when one considers the prevalence and accessibility of music listening. Also, it is easier to measure a person's responses while he is listening to music than while he is performing it.

The trend to objectively measure the effects of music began full force in the 1930s, and was largely influenced by the search for scientific proof which was occurring in other areas of medicine, psychotherapy, and rehabilitation. Much of the data on the effects of music on mind, body, spirit, and emotions have been organized according to whether the music presented to listeners is stimulative or sedative. Stimulative music has been described as emphasizing "rhythm rather than melody or harmony and is characterized by loud, staccato passages with wide pitch ranges and abrupt, unpredictable changes." Sedative music "emphasizes melody and harmony more than rhythm and is characterized by soft, legato passages with narrow pitch ranges and gradual, predictable changes."[2] Fast, slow, driving, or leisurely tempo may also impact a person's experience of music as either stimulative or sedative.

Since most genres of music have some range of tempo, dynamic level, consonance, dissonance, and melodic structure, examples of stimulative and sedative music may be found in just about any form of music. Rock, classical, ethnic, jazz, and country and western all have pieces that may be characterized as stimulative or sedative. Although researchers originally believed that generalizations about the effects of music on people would be based on whether the music presented was stimulative or sedative, actual findings have been rather inconsistent, which is probably due to variables that have little to do with the music itself.

For example, the instrumentation, performer, or interpretation of the same piece of music may affect its perception as either stimulative or sedative. Also, often depending upon their previous experience with music, different people may experience "stimulative" or "sedative" in different ways, making an objective measure of these terms difficult. Still, the individual perception of the stimulative or sedative nature of music remains a crucial variable in assessing the effects of music.

• Listen to What You Like

Another significant variable in understanding the effect of music is personal preference. Research shows that your responses to music are strongly influenced by your like or dislike of the particular music you hear. Take opera and disco, as extreme examples: Some may experience opera as relaxing, while others may grow increasingly agitated simply because they do not enjoy this type of music. The same holds true for disco: Some may find it fun, energizing, and joyful, while others may experience physical and/or emotional discomfort as a result of listening to it.

Since preference is so important in determining responses to music, a brief review of research will help you understand why you choose the music you do, so you can maximize the positive results from listening experiences. Studies have shown that familiarity, repetition, and training are strong contributors to musical preference, and that repeated hearing of particular pieces increased the tendency to prefer those pieces. A person's knowledge about the recent work of Dr. Helen Bonny, a music therapist who has devoted much of her career to the study of the effects of music listening on people. Her recent study of music listening in intensive-coronary-care units demonstrated that "physiological measures from pre to post music listening for each patient showed . . . a highly significant decrease in heart rate" when patients listened to sedative music tapes of either classical or popular music.[3]

The research on the relationship between respiration rate (how fast or slow you breathe in and out) and music shows that respiration increases with stimulative music and decreases with sedative music, increases with either stimulative or sedative music, or increases only if a person enjoys whatever music he is listening to.[4] Similar varying results have been found in the relationship between music listening and the rise and fall of blood pressure. Recent work in this area has also come from Dr. Bonny. Her carefully designed sedative listening programs have been demonstrated to produce a "trend toward decrease of both systolic and diastolic blood pressure measures."[5] This finding points to the potential exciting use of music as a valuable treatment aid in the management of high blood pressure, a growing health concern in society today.

The dilation of the pupils of the eyes has also been studied in relation to music listening. Sedative music often causes pupilary constriction, while stimulative music tends to produce pupilary dilation. This finding is interesting when you consider that pupil dilation is a way of taking in, while constriction is a way of shutting out. Perhaps stimulative music causes us to literally wake up and take in more from the environment, while sedative music produces more relaxation and less of a need to attend to the outer world.

Gastric (stomach) contractions can also be affected by music. Sedative music has been found to increase the intensity and regularity of contractions, while stimulative music causes just the opposite. Contractions will cease altogether when an individual is displeased with the music being heard.[6]

Many physical responses that are not rhythmic in nature, such as muscle tension, may also be affected by music. A logical assumption is that listening to a "tense" piece of music will cause corresponding tension in the body. Similarly, we can assume that an easing of physical tension accompanies listening to flowing, relaxing music. Support for this idea comes from two studies. In one,

the music being heard also tended to create preference for that music.[3] Stated simply, people tend to prefer music that they know about, hear often, and understand.

The relationship between personality and musical preference as a way to understand our individual likes and dislikes in music has also been studied. One researcher found a positive relationship between the personality traits of unconventionality and radicalism and a taste for electronic music.[4] Think about how the music you like may reflect your personality.

Other studies have shown that:

- Sex *is not* a predictor of musical preference.[5] Despite some popular beliefs, women do not consistently prefer different kinds of music than men, and vice versa.
- Age *is* often a predictor of musical preference.[6] A study of school-aged children indicated that they preferred rock music to classical as their age increased. This finding may help explain changes in your music preferences over the years.
- Race, social class, and political orientation *may be* a predictor of musical preference, and vice versa.[7] People often prefer music of their own cultural group for a variety of emotional, social, or religious reasons. People also tend to prefer music that supports their political beliefs or social status. An example of this is the political protest music of the 1960s, which was supported by many young people as a statement of their beliefs and ideologies.[8] In addition, some forms of music are more accessible to the wealthy than to the poor. Unfortunately, this often results in reinforcing musical preferences that have been determined by social and economic factors.

Another variable to consider in studying the effects of music listening is the elusive nature of music. The musical moment occurs and then is gone, and each moment brings a new and ever-changing response in the complete musical experience. Further, no two performances of the same piece are ever the same. Even the same performer tends to vary the interpretation of a piece during different performances, making generalizations about the effects of that piece, beyond the actual moment it is occurring, difficult to determine. Also, the environment in which you listen to music may alter your responses. Who you are with, the acoustics of the concert hall, and the temperature of the room are but a few things to consider. In addition, your own internal environment is in constant flux. How you are feeling emotionally or physically may dramatically affect your receptivity to music at any given moment. The events in your life just prior to a music-listening experience will also color your response. A quarrel with a loved one just before a concert may negatively impact your ability to relax and enjoy the music. On the other hand, the music may be just the thing to soothe frazzled nerves.

As people have attempted to determine the ways in which music affects us, they have been continually challenged by these variables. However, studying what findings there are on the effects of music listening on our physical, mental, emotional, and spiritual selves, in spite of various research difficulties, can still help you to learn more about yourself and music.

In the next four sections, we will consider what is known about music and mind, mood, body, and spirit. As you read these sections, think about your own responses to music. You may find some similarities, differences, or new directions to explore. Keep in mind that your *own* preference is the most crucial aspect of how music will affect you. By listening to the music you like, you can make music work for you, and attain positive results in your life.

14
Let's Get Physical! Music for the Body

Music has long been believed to have powerful effect body. For many of us, this is logical and easily und The inherent rhythmic nature of our bodily processes, in with the rhythm of our lives, makes us naturally resp music on the physical level. In fact, as discussed in Cha is through our bodies that we first respond to the rhythm

Most of the studies on the effects of music on our bc looked at how music affects our physiological rhythms. T of stimulative and sedative music on heart rate and have been the most common areas of investigation. Th normal heart rate is 72–80 beats per minute. Interes is the same as the average tempo of most of Western what Handel called "tempo gusto!" This tempo has found to directly correspond to our normal reaction t a second, which is also the duration of a complete perception. This time value is in many ways, therefor and physiological constant in our lives.

The exact effect of music on your heart rate and unclear. Some studies have shown that both rates in stimulative music, some that they decrease with sed and still others that they increase with *either* stimulativ music.[1] This last finding may be due to the fact that experience is inherently stimulating in some way. (have shown no effect in either direction, or unpred from trial to trial.[2] In addition, many of the results levels of statistical significance. An exception to th

the separate and combined effects of progressive muscle relaxation (PMR) and music listening were investigated to determine which best induced relaxation.[7] Although both music and PMR were effective separately in reducing stress, the combination of music and PMR was even more effective.

The other study was related to the effect of music on muscle strength and hand grip. People's grip strength was measured while they were listening to stimulative music, sedative music, and silence. Findings showed that grip strength decreased with sedative music, as compared with silence. Stimulative music and silence had no effect on increasing or decreasing grip strength.[8] This study has important clues for those who enjoy exercising to music. Due to its relaxing nature, sedative music might have a negative impact on someone exercising with free weights, Nautilus equipment, or other programs that require a strong grip. Stimulative music (or even silence) may not increase your grip, but it will certainly not detract from your workout.

The newest frontier of research on the physical effects of music listening is in the field of pain management. Music has been found to be effective in reducing pain in dental procedures, surgery, childbirth, and various other medical situations.[9] When used in this way, the music is called "audioanalgesia," and explanations as to how music relieves pain are fairly consistent among studies.

Since pain is often an expression of stress and muscular tension, any medium that brings about relaxation may be considered beneficial for you. During pain management, music has been used to effectively bring about relaxation and divert attention from either the pain or the anxiety aroused by hospital sounds. In cancer wards and intensive-coronary-care units, music listening has been found to increase patients' tolerance of pain and suffering and, at times, reduce the need for pain medication.[10] One explanation for this occurrence is that calming, quiet music may help produce peptides—molecules that relieve pain through their action in the brain.[11] Music in conjunction with verbal instructions for relaxation has also been very effective in the treatment of pain. Studies suggest that "auditory stimulation [music], together with a strong suggestion that the music would indeed abolish pain, provided an effective stratagem for achieving control over . . . slowly rising pain."[12]

The use of music with verbal instruction has been especially successful in reducing pain during childbirth. In some instances, this routinely lowers the amount of anesthesia required and often shortens labor.[13] In two recent studies, pregnant women instructed in Lamaze techniques were assisted by music therapists in preparing audio tapes for labor and delivery.[14] The music selections were based on the mother's preferences for music and observations of her breathing in response to the selections. The tapes usually included stimulative as well as sedative music, depending on the mother's needs at different points in the labor and delivery process. For example, music with increased tempo, intensity, and energy was often used for the later stages of labor, in order to aid the mother in pushing with contractions.

According to the therapists who participated in these studies, music has the potential to promote relaxation, trigger positive associations, divert attention from the pain and anxiety-provoking sounds, and cue rhythmic breathing. Music also provides a sense of support during this stressful physical experience, similar to the support people feel when exercising to music. In one study, one hundred percent of the mothers who participated displayed less pain while the music was playing than while it was not. Enthusiastic responses from participants included "I couldn't have made it without the music" and "We were all brought together in a musical celebration of life."[15]

Positive feedback from the medical staff about the presence of music in the hospital setting was also received in the course of these studies. Bonny has suggested that music be played in nurses' and doctors' lounges, to aid in reducing their stress and tension. Other reports of the use of music by doctors in the operating room to provide a pleasant, less stressful environment are becoming more common.[16]

• Your Body and Music

Research shows that music *does* have a definite physiological impact upon us, though what its exact effects are, under what circumstances they occur, and what type of music is most effective are currently unpredictable. Therefore, observation of your own preferences and responses to music is the best guide when using music for physical reasons. Before beginning any plan for physical change with music, however, remember that it can have a potent impact on your body. For this reason, it is important that you *not* use music for the self-treatment of such diagnosed medical conditions as high blood pressure, heart conditions, respiratory ailments, and so on. The research cited in this chapter has been presented solely for purposes of informing the reader about certain known effects of music on the body, *not* of suggesting he or she use such information to treat any condition deserving of medical attention. Music may be beneficial in treating such conditions, but only under the supervision of your physician and in consultation with a trained music therapist. For now, we will use the information from this research in a limited way to guide your development of a music program to improve physical conditions that *do not require medical assistance.*

To begin your program of music listening for physical improvement, you will need to spend some time listening to different kinds of music in order to learn what you experience as stimulative or sedative. To determine this, pay close attention to your breathing, pulse rate, and muscular tension before and after your listening experience. Sometimes the physiological effects of music are immediately noticeable; other times they take a while to appear. Therefore, allow yourself about twenty minutes with a particular piece or type of music to ensure maximum awareness of its effects on you. Choose music that you like, and remember that personal preference is an important factor in how you will respond to music.

You will probably find it useful to extend your exploration over a period of time in order to find out what kinds of music work best for you during different times of the day, week, or month. You may want to try exercising to different types of music before deciding on what is best for you, or take a few weeks of experimentation to find the right music for relaxation. Time is also important to consider when planning for physical change through music. Some people may be able to immediately relax to music, while others may need an hour or more of listening time to fully experience the music's effects.

• Let Your Body Listen

You are now ready to begin determining your responses to music. Just follow these easy steps:

Exercise 14-1

Find a comfortable position for listening, either sitting or lying down, in a place free from noises and other distractions. Select a piece of music you like and feel especially attracted to listening to at this moment.

As you get ready to listen, check in with your physical self so that you may later determine whether you experienced the music as stimulative or sedative. An easy way to begin is to check your pulse rate. Place a hand on either your wrist or your neck, count the number of beats for ten seconds, then multiply by six, and you will have your pulse rate. Now check your breathing. Is it fast, slow, or normal for you? How about your muscular tension or posture? Do your shoulders feel tight? Are you experiencing pain or stiffness anywhere? Do you feel rubbery and loose and almost as if you could fall asleep right now?

Now tell yourself that you will allow your body to experience the effects of the music you will hear. There is no right or wrong to this experience, only your own natural responses. You are now ready to listen to the music you have chosen.

As you listen, let your body respond as it wishes. You may find that you want to sit up, lie down, clap, hum along, or even get up and dance around the room. Let yourself do whatever comes. Continue to pay attention to what is happening to your breathing and pulse. You may also note your feelings and thoughts about the music and any associations it may bring, since they are probably related to your physical state.

When the music is over, check in with yourself again. What changes, if any, do you notice? Take your pulse again to see if it has quickened, slowed, or stayed the same. Check your breathing and muscular tension. Note the position you are in compared with the one you assumed when you first began listening. How would you describe yourself right now? Tense? Relaxed? Stimulated? Sleepy?

You may use this exercise as a model for determining your different physical responses to music. Once you have assessed your responses to the stimulative and sedative effects of different kinds of music over a period of time, you are ready to begin purposively using music for relaxation or stimulation, to achieve positive physical results.

• Balancing Tension and Relaxation

Under healthful conditions there is a natural balance of tension and relaxation in our bodies. The simplest example of this is the ongoing tension and relaxation of our muscles when we walk or lift something. Physical difficulties often arise when this balance is thrown out of kilter for some reason, as in an overworked muscle that is unable to relax, or an underworked muscle that is unable to provide the necessary tension to work effectively. A similar balance of tension and relaxation also exists in the nonphysical aspects of our lives. It is important for us to be alert and stimulated in order to work, and equally important for us to rest and relax. The appropriate balance between the two leads to a productive and healthy life.

Music listening is a powerful and accessible way to achieve a balance of physical stimulation and relaxation in our lives. Since you have different needs for physical arousal or relaxation at different times, you can learn what music to use when, in order to enhance your natural physical functioning. For physical stimulation, you may easily add music to your life as an accompaniment to exercise or dancing and to increase physical energy and motivation. For relaxation, the right music may help you fall asleep more easily at bedtime, or reduce stress after a long day at the office.

• Exercising to Music

Music is a natural accompaniment to almost any exercise program. In fact, it is rare to see people exercising *without* music. Many people jog with their personal tape players or radios, and most health clubs have music piped into their exercise rooms. Classes in aerobic dancing and jazzercise use music as an integral part of exercise routines.

The reasons for including music in exercise are simple. Both music and exercise involve rhythm, tempo, and movement. The rhythm and tempo of a piece of music may help cue the timing and pacing of movements, such as leg lifts, sit-ups, or stretches. The movement of music over time corresponds to the movement of the body through a particular exercise sequence or pattern. Music may also help cue deep and regular breathing, crucial to the success of any exercise program. A healthy supply of oxygen helps ward off sore muscles, cramps, exhaustion, and a feeling of depletion at the end of your workout.

Both music and exercise involve harmony. Through music, you can experience the blend of different instruments, sounds, and rhythms into a harmonious whole. Through exercise, you can experience the blend of your different rhythms and movements in a harmonious physical concert. Running, swimming, or aerobic dancing in perfect time with yourself to just the right music often provides an exhilarating sense of internal and external harmony.

Many people find that listening to music during exercise breaks the monotony, helps the time go by faster, and lessens the discomfort of a workout by providing a pleasant distraction. A recent study of runners and music listening supports this. The runners interviewed reported that running "seemed easier" when they listened to upbeat music than when they ran at the same pace without the music. Physiological tests on heart rate and changes in body chemistry indicated that the runners were working just as hard on each trial. However, measures of endorphins, the opiate-like chemicals that the body produces under many stressful conditions, were lower when the runners listened to music than when they did not. Thus, the *feeling* that music made the exercise easier actually altered the body chemistry of participants in this study.[17]

In looking for the right exercise music for you, choose music that fits the tempo and pace of your workout. Music that is interesting to hear and physically stimulating without being stressful will enhance your exercise. Find a good variety of music to use, since listening to the same music each week will add to, rather than lessen, the monotony of your program. Rock and roll may feel good for exercise one day but maybe not the next. Also, even if you are not directly in control of the music in your exercise environment, you can have a say in what you are hearing. Ask your health-club manager to change the radio station or tape if the music is particularly uncomfortable to you. Or let your exercise teacher know which music does and does not help motivate you in class. Exercise time may also provide an opportunity to listen to new kinds of music, if your schedule does not allow for this exploration at home.

SUGGESTIONS

If you need some suggestions to help you get started with music for exercise, try the following recordings. Remember to monitor your own responses and use these only as suggestions or a starting place for finding what is right for you.

1. *Flashdance*—soundtrack from the motion picture, Polygram Records.
2. *Running on Empty,* by Jackson Browne, Asylum Records.
3. *Suite for Flute and Jazz Piano,* by Jean-Pierre Rampal and Claude Bolling, Columbia Records.
4. Bach's Brandenburg Concerto No. 2 in F, RCA Records.

Also, make good use of your radio in your exploration. Listen to many different stations for a variety of styles and types of music to find what works for you.

Other factors to consider when using music to enhance exercise are the environment, season, and climate. For example, a friend of ours brought a rock-and-roll tape along for a jog on a serene country road one day. She found that the music was too dissonant for the surroundings. In this instance, a classical tape would have better suited her run. Another friend found that listening to popular, jazz, or rock music while running in hot, humid summer weather actually increased her stress. Classical music seemed to diminish the heat and create a more satisfying run. Still another friend told us that he prefers not to listen to music at all while running, because he feels that the music prevents him from making contact with his own rhythm. The rhythmic pounding of his own feet and the sound of his breathing are all the music he needs for a successful workout.

• Dancing and Motivating with Music

Dancing is another way many people exercise, get motivated, and experience the physical benefits of music listening. Dancing often meets our needs for rhythmic contact with ourselves and others.

It can ward off physical boredom and provide stimulation and entertainment for our bodies. The desire to get up and dance is a natural response to music. We derive pleasure and gratification from moving to music, much as, in infancy, we enjoyed being rocked and held, or bounced on someone's knee.

Our natural need to move is another form of self-expression and communication, similar to our need to make sounds and be heard by others. Dance is a more developed form of this early behavior, and an important way in which we are physically nurtured by music. Although many people believe they "can't dance," anyone can move to music. Dancing can be anything from highly stylized ballroom or disco patterns to your own creative movements in the privacy of your living room. Whatever you choose, remember that your natural inclinations to move to music are healthy physical expressions of you.

Music may also be used to enhance your overall sense of physical energy and motivation. Quick, lively music can energize your body to move through chores in the same way it can help you to move through an exercise routine. Increases in heart rate, pulse rate, and respiratory rate caused by stimulative music naturally induce greater physical activity, just as decreases in these functions eventually lead to relaxation and sleep.

• Relaxing with Music

Physical relaxation is as crucial to your health as physical stimulation. Through relaxation, your body becomes nurtured and revitalized and ready to once again face the physical demands of work and play. Body pain, muscle tension, and fatigue are all expressions of an overworked physical system.

Just as you experimented with music for physical stimulation, begin to explore music that you find physically relaxing in a number of ways. Your needs for relaxation to music will probably vary from day to day. Sometimes you may wish to use music to help you relax into sleep; other times more specifically to help relieve a stiff back or tension headache. You may also use music to help keep you calm while stuck in a traffic jam or before an anxiety-producing business situation. Whatever your need, remember that care of your physical self will have a positive impact on your whole self.

You might want to try the following recordings in your search for the right relaxing music for you:

1. *Tarashanti,* by Georgia Kelly, Heru Records.
2. *Passages,* by William Ackerman, Windham Hill Records.
3. *Segovia on Stage* (classical guitar music), by Andrés Segovia, Decca Gold Label Records.

Learning to relax to music involves only time and experimentation. Different from many relaxation techniques that require you to recline or to be in an environment conducive to completion of specific exercises, music is a go-anywhere tool for relaxation, ready to use in a variety of personal and professional settings. Here are some points to keep in mind while you're listening:

1. *Use music that evokes pleasant associations, memories, thoughts, or images.* Many people find music that reminds them of nature or water to be particularly soothing and relaxing.
2. *Use music that helps you breathe regularly and deeply.* Respiration is an extremely important part of pain and stress management. When we are anxious or in pain, we tend to stop breathing. This is the body's way of cutting off uncomfortable sensations, but in fact it creates greater discomfort, as diminished oxygen intake increases the body's sense of emergency or crisis. Breathing is the key to relaxation and release.
3. *Use music that diverts your attention from the source of pain, anxiety, or tension.* Concentrate instead on the music and your breathing.
4. *As you are listening, remind yourself that music is a natural source of comfort, nurturance, and healing.* By breathing and listening fully, you will be replenishing and rejuvenating aching muscles and stressed limbs.
5. *If you are in physical distress that impairs your functioning in any way, seek the appropriate medical attention and consult with a music therapist if you wish music to be a part of your treatment program.*

Finally, music is an effective way to balance and stabilize our ongoing needs for physical stimulation and relaxation. Since you can bring music with you almost anywhere, it is an ideal form of self-help for your body. Whether you are in your car, on a plane, away from home, at work, or lying on a beach, music is available for your physical needs. It is on when you want it, off when you don't. It is safe, nonmedicinal, and when played at comfortable volumes has no known side effects other than the enrichment of your life. There are few other physical remedies that can claim so much. Perhaps the day will come when a common prescription for physical ailments will be "Take two sonatas and call me in the morning."

15
What a Feeling! Music for the Emotions

After physical responses, your most natural and common response to music is through your emotions. That music can move you to joy, sorrow, or grief is a well-known fact of life. Through the ages, music has always accompanied every deeply emotional human experience, from mourning to celebration. People have long used music to express what is inexpressible in words, and all music serves the function of stimulating, expressing, and showing emotion.[1]

Our emotional responses to music are based on our experiences with sound in infancy and childhood. Our early rhythmic and melodic exchanges with others, particularly our mothers, form one of the strongest emotional bonds of our lives. We express our most primary emotions of happiness, anger, sadness, and fear through sound-making. The inherent musicality of these expressions makes us acutely sensitive to the emotional quality of similar sounds in music, such as the "cry" of a violin, the "laughter" of a flute, or the "groan" of a tuba.

A clear example of the emotional content of music is found in love songs, which comprise the major portion of all popular music. The enduring nature of love songs in every generation indicates that people enjoy and need these expressions of love lost, found, and unrequited. In fact, a popular radio station in New York City is able to devote all its programming to "love songs . . . nothing but love songs."[2] People seem to enjoy listening to love songs because they hear their own experiences in them. When lovers find "their song," it is usually because it is reminiscent of a particular time, place, or event in their relationship when their emotions were at a high pitch. The song then becomes a symbol of those feelings and can help to continually re-create memories of them.

All music, whether or not a love song, expresses emotion and evokes emotion within us. This process begins when an individual is so moved by an event, person, place, or experience that he is inspired to write a piece of music or sing a song. When that music is shared with others, the listeners are invited to empathize with the composer's experience and emotions and add their own. The listeners may also experience validation of their own emotions in the music, often an important part in determining preferences for particular pieces. Just as people respond more favorably to music that validates their internal rhythmic state, they also respond favorably to music that corresponds to their emotional state. Thus, when people sway, nod, smile, or cry to music, they are often saying "Yes—this music speaks to my experience. I feel what this music is saying."

Primary to the process of expressing and evoking emotion in music is our basic need to communicate and be understood by others. As discussed in Chapter 1, the act of hearing and being heard is one of the most emotionally significant aspects of our early life. Our feelings are often what we most want others to hear, and when they do, we are free to hear their feelings and respond as well. Without this opportunity to experience our emotions, have them heard by others, and feel empathy toward the emotional experiences of others, our lives become empty.

Music is a powerful way in which you can experience a healthy flow of empathy. Listening to music helps you hear and understand another's emotional experience, as well as validate your own experience and mood. As discussed earlier, Susanne Langer believes that music resonates so powerfully with our emotions because both exist as dynamic forms, constantly changing, moving, and existing only in time.[3] The ability to fully feel our emotions, in all their meaning and dynamic form in an even flow over time, leads to a healthy and poignant approach to life. Unchanging emotions, such as prolonged anger, sadness, or fear, cause discomfort and a "stuck" approach to life. In music, this would be equivalent to an unchanging tone and rhythm. At first it may sound interesting and seem to be going somewhere, yet, as it persists, it becomes less meaningful.

Another explanation for the deep connection between music

and emotions comes from research on the human brain. Scientists studying the similarities, differences, and relationships between the brain's two hemispheres have discovered that although sensory input is received by both halves of the brain, it is dealt with differently in each. The left hemisphere seems to process input in verbal, logical, and analytic ways. Thus, the ability to communicate through words, think through a problem, or figure a math equation are all left-hemisphere functions. In contrast, the right hemisphere seems to be your nonverbal, metaphoric, intuitive, imaginative, and emotional side. Research has shown that much of music is processed through the right side of the brain. Loss of right-hemisphere functioning due to a stroke or other disability causes the inability to sing, adequately remember music, or recognize musical sounds. Left-hemisphere dysfunction often results in an inability to speak, although the individual may still sing and fully understand and appreciate music.[4]

Different music activities involve one or both sides of the brain. Reading music and translating these notes onto an instrument are left-hemisphere tasks. The feeling, interpretation, or emotion that is added by the performer is a right-hemisphere function. Listening to a piece of music and analyzing the tonal structures or performance technique is a left-hemisphere occurrence; being moved to tears by the sound of a piece is a right-hemisphere event. Using both sides of the brain during listening or playing music is also possible, as in reading notes and performing them with "feeling," or knowing the names of the chords you are hearing and feeling moved by their sound. Without the right side of your brain, much of your connection to music is lost.

• Music and Your Moods

The secret to predicting emotional responses to music has long captivated the interest of researchers. Unlocking this secret holds important implications for your use of music as a tool in creating emotional well-being.

Kate Hevner, an early researcher in the connection between emotion and music, sought to isolate aspects of music that correspond to particular mood states. In her research, individuals were asked to listen to selected pieces of music and choose from a selected list those adjectives that best illustrated the mood of the music to them. From their responses, Hevner theorized that the perception of emotion in music was most influenced by the tempo, modality, and pitch level of the music, and less by the harmony, rhythm, and melodic direction.[5] The product of this research is Hevner's "mood wheel," a listing of sixty-six adjectives in eight related groups that classify the possible emotional attributes of a piece of music.[6] Take a moment now and look over Hevner's mood wheel (page 177) and imagine that these adjectives are arranged around an imaginary circle. You will notice that groups right next to one another are related, while diagonally opposite groups are quite unrelated. The progression around the circle from group 1 to group 8 represents the full range of human emotions. We will return to this mood wheel later on and show you how to use it to change your moods with music.

Dr. Helen Bonny has studied Hevner's mood wheel and used it to determine the moods communicated by particular musical selections. She also asked people to listen to a selection and then check the adjective group they felt corresponded to the mood of the music. Many of the pieces were found to produce the same choice among the listeners. The results of her studies indicate a strong relationship between a piece and the moods many people will attribute to it. For example, *Appalachian Spring,* by Aaron Copland, was consistently categorized within group 4, while *Jesus Christ Superstar,* by Webber and Rice, was consistently categorized within group 6.[7]

An important point to consider in viewing this work is that associating emotional qualities with a piece of music does not imply that the listener is *experiencing* those emotions *while* listening. Although we frequently feel emotional while listening to music, it is also possible for us to empathize with the emotion *without* experiencing it. This is similar to our ability to understand a friend's emotion without at the same time experiencing that emotion.

Other research about music and emotions has specifically to do with anxiety, aggression, and stress. These three feelings have been found to be a result of listening to stimulative, rather than sedative, music. In one study, music described as "exciting" produced more anxiety and aggression than calm music.[8] Other studies found that college students who listened to stimulative music before an exam experienced increased anxiety, as compared with students who listened to sedative music or to no music at all.[9]

Arrangement of Adjectives for Recording
the Mood Effect of Music

6

merry
joyous
gay

7

exhilarated
soaring
triumphant
dramatic
passionate
sensational
agitated
exciting
impetuous
restless

happy
cheerful
bright

5

humorous
playful
whimsical
fanciful
quaint
sprightly
delicate
light
graceful

8

vigorous
robust
emphatic
martial
ponderous
majestic
exalting

4

lyrical
leisurely
satisfying
serene
tranquil
quiet
soothing

1

spiritual
lofty
awe-inspiring
dignified
sacred
solemn
sober
serious

2

pathetic
doleful
sad
mournful
tragic
melancholy
frustrated
depressing
gloomy
heavy
dark

3

dreamy
yielding
tender
sentimental
longing
yearning
pleading
plaintive

Certainly the perception of stimulative and sedative music is highly individual, and not all stimulative music will lead you to feel anxiety, aggression, or stress. Still, these studies may help you understand some of your responses to particular types of music, and guide you toward using music to manage day-to-day anxiety and other stress-related emotions. Since exciting or stimulative music has been found, at times, to increase anxiety, you might want to avoid it when facing stressful situations. To combat stress and anxiety, try listening to music that you find calming and sedative.

Although particular pieces or types of music often produce common emotional responses among people, your personal preference continues to be the single most important factor in determining your emotional responses to music. Other factors to be considered are your personality, mood set, personal association to the words (if any), and physical environment while you're listening. The strength of the emotion you may feel—even such an "unpleasant" emotion as sadness—will be directly related to your like or dislike of the piece you are hearing.

Convenient as it would be to be able to prescribe or suggest specific pieces of music for specific emotional results, this would not take into account your individual nuances and preferences for music. Emotional responses to music are highly personal, and it is very common for different people to have different, even opposite, emotional reactions to the same piece of music. In many ways this is part of the beauty, richness, and wonder of music.

• Moving Moods

Even though we may not always be able to predict another's emotional responses to music, it has been proven that we can change our own mood by listening to music. This is explained by the iso-moodic principle. According to this principle, your mood can be altered by first matching the music to your existing mood and then gradually changing the mood of the music in the direction you wish to change.[10] Thus, if you are feeling sad and wish to be happy, begin by listening to music that you experience as sad. Although this may seem to reinforce your sadness, acknowledgment of what you feel is the first step in any attempt to change.

The iso-moodic principle is simple in concept and requires only your time, knowledge of your emotional responses to music, and willingness to use music for emotional change. Let's return to the example of sadness. Look at Hevner's mood wheel (page 177) and map out a progression from sadness to happiness around the circle. Move from "sad" (group 2) to "dreamy" (group 3) to "lyrical" (group 4) to "playful" (group 5) to "happy" (group 6).

Begin by listening to a sad piece and then to pieces that represent each group to you. By listening to music in this progression, you will ease yourself out of sadness and into a more pleasant-feeling state. The amount of music you will need to listen to in each category will depend on the intensity of your mood when you began, your willingness to change your mood, and your openness to using music as a vehicle for this change.

The iso-moodic principle may be implemented to change any number of moods, such as "agitated" to "quiet," "vigorous" to "tranquil," "frustrated" to "playful," and so on. The most important things to remember are to begin by acknowledging your present state and then move *gradually* toward your final goal. Too abrupt a change can result in discomfort similar to that one feels upon seeing bright light just after sleeping, or plunging into ice-cold water after sunbathing. Just as you would allow your eyes to become accustomed to the light, or ease yourself into the swimming pool, allow your emotions time to change toward something new. Using the iso-moodic principle is a natural and healthful way to produce emotional change, which requires only your time, some experimentation, and a basic record or tape collection. In fact, while reading along, you may have discovered that you have been naturally using this iso-moodic principle to help you maintain or alter your moods.

Awareness of the relationship between music and your emotions will help you use music to create emotional well-being. Music can add a richness to your emotional life which may be experienced anywhere, anytime, anyplace, and with anyone you choose. By simply opening your ears and your heart, you can accept music's invitation into the world of emotional experience, expression, and expansion.

16

Mind over Music: Music to Think By

Along with our natural physical and emotional responses to music, we spend a significant amount of time thinking about the music we hear, discussing it with friends, planning music experiences, learning about and through music. Certainly performers spend many hours thinking about music, developing their skills, and attuning their minds to the intellectual aspects of study and performance. Yet, even for nonprofessionals, the mind is an important part of fully experiencing music. The most obvious effects of music on your mind are the thoughts, associations, and memories that come to you when you're listening to it. The familiar strains of "Here Comes the Bride" or "Jingle Bells" are simple examples of how you immediately connect experiences and events to music. In fact, music is so evocative of memories, thoughts, and associations that music therapists have long known the value of music in treating senility, disorientation, and loss of memory among the elderly.

The ways in which people choose to use music for their mind are varied. Some people consciously pursue the intellectual aspects of music through analysis of form, structure, and harmony. Others may choose to let their minds wander to a particular scene, real or imagined, while listening to music. Still others find that music helps them to concentrate on a specific task, to study, or to solve a problem. People also often use music as an *escape* from thinking, and allow themselves to bask in the spiritual, sensual, physical, or emotional aspects of listening. Each of these choices is a valid means of experiencing music's impact on your mind.

Much of the relationship between music and your mind is deter-mined by your social and cultural background. Since music is a form of communication, it transmits meaning. Your understanding of the intended musical meaning is often the result of your exposure to and experience with this system of communication, similar to your ability to make meaning out of a foreign language. For this reason, it is not uncommon to hear people say that they do not understand music from a different culture, or even generation. What this implies is merely a lack of knowledge about the music, which may be overcome through positive and informed listening experiences.

Other aspects of understanding music are related to your prior experiences and learning. We *think* of a wedding when we hear "Here Comes the Bride," because that is where we most often hear this piece. For the same reason, we immediately associate mourning with a piece entitled "Funeral March." Similarly, your thought about a type of music may *affect* your experience of it. If you *think* classical music is boring, chances are you will experience it in this way, unless you consciously choose to open your mind to a new experience. Many people have also closed themselves off from music because they *think* they are untalented or have had negative experiences with music in the past. What we think about music often affects how we will hear music, and vice versa.

In this chapter, we invite you to open your mind to new thoughts, experiences, and ideas about the world of music. An expanded cognitive approach to music represents expansion of the whole self. As you read on in this section, think about your attitudes, beliefs, and thoughts about music, and give yourself permission to explore the exercises we will suggest for opening your mind through music.

• The Mind's Eye and Ear

Synesthesia is a fascinating example of the connection between mind and music. This is a condition in which stimulation of one sense arouses imagery in another. Synesthesia is found in the comment "It looks cold outside." In this instance, our visual sense produces imagery about heat or coldness. An example of synesthesia and music is known as "colored hearing." This occurs when individuals hear music and see or sense color at the same time. Other examples of synesthesia and music would be drawing a representation of the music one has heard, or composing a piece of music in response to a visual experience.

Illustrations of synesthesia and music abound in verbalizations about music. Using such words as *cool, rough, sharp, smooth, blue, light,* and *airy* to describe music is an example of how we do this. Marshall McLuhan suggests that listening to live music is necessarily a synesthetic experience when he says: "To be in the presence of performing musicians is to experience their touch and handling of the instruments as tactile and kinetic, not just resonant."[1]

One of the most common forms of synesthesia is the experiencing of visual images in response to sounds or music. An example of this is the sense of brightness in response to pitch. For instance: "Thunder, drums, deep voices and low-pitched sounds in general produce dark images, whereas squeaks, violins, soprano voices and other high-pitched sounds produce white or bright images."[2] In addition, it is common for people to find that as pitch rises, brightness increases. Pitch also appears to affect the size and shape of the images that are evoked. High pitches generally evoke images that are small, angular, and sharply edged. Lower pitches tend to evoke images that are dark, round, or massive. The dynamic level also affects visual images, such that soft sounds produce dim images and loud sounds produce bright images.

As you are reading, you are probably recalling some of your own synesthetic experiences with music. Symphonic program music, such as Tchaikovsky's *Nutcracker Suite,* is renowned for its use of the elements of music and orchestration to create synesthetic perceptions and visual imagery. This is clearly illustrated in a description of Vivaldi's *Four Seasons* by Martin Bookspan:

> Birds are heard twittering in trills that alternate between the solo violin and the violins of the orchestra. A murmuring stream is heard in rushing figures in the lower strings and there are flashes of lightning in the violins and claps of thunder in the broken chords of the solo violin.[3]

The image of a waterfall in response to a descending melody in a flowing tempo, the picture of a bird from the trill of a piccolo, or a sense of darkness and impending doom in response to the low drone of a tympani are just a few of the ways in which you may have experienced synesthesia and music.

Related to synesthesia is a music-therapy technique known as Guided Imagery and Music (GIM), developed by Dr. Helen Bonny. Under the guidance of a trained facilitator, participants in this treatment are placed in states of deep relaxation while listening to live or taped music, and are encouraged to let their personal imagery, thoughts, sensations, or associations evoked by the music emerge, in an effort to resolve personal conflicts, reduce stress, gain greater personal insight, or heighten spirituality. During a GIM session, it is not uncommon for people to experience colors, images, bodily sensations, and even elaborate fantasies in response to the music. As Dr. Bonny notes, "music seems to acquire color, shape, motion—even taste and scent . . . melodies, harmonies and rhythms reveal meanings; insights into self are a common occurrence, one sees more ways to look at a problem, an idea, a person."[4]

• Seeing the Music You Hear

Although GIM is intended for use as a therapeutic tool with a trained therapist, you can experience synesthesia and imagery with music through simple and relaxing listening experiences. Relaxation is important, since imagery is more likely to arise if you are in a relaxed state. To begin your own exploration of the effects of music and your mind, choose one of your favorite pieces of music for the following exercise:

Exercise 16-1

Choose a piece that is at least fifteen to twenty minutes long. You may choose a vocal or nonvocal piece, but keep in mind that the words of the music will probably affect your imagery, thoughts, and associations in some way. The music may be any type you wish, and either stimulative or sedative. Also, since the title of the piece, words of the music, or specific elements of the orchestration or structure may suggest the composer's intention, give yourself permission to allow *your* own imagery and meanings to emerge.

Before you begin to listen, take a moment to relax. Breathe deeply, find a comfortable position for listening, and tell yourself that you will let your mind openly respond to the music.

Close your eyes and let yourself experience whatever your mind is creating in response to the music, whether it be recounting an experience from work, reliving a childhood memory, or visiting a happy yet forgotten place. As you are listening and responding to the music, flow with your mind and the pictures or sensations you are creating.

As the piece comes to a close, begin to put an ending on the thought, fantasy, or image you have created.

Afterward, take some time to think about the exercise. You may even want to write down your experience as a way to help you process what you thought or felt. Did you decide how to end a quarrel with a friend or a lover? Come up with a new idea for rearranging your apartment? Envision your next vacation? Determine that perfect gift for a friend's birthday? Think back now to how the music helped activate this mental process. Did the music evoke color, which then reminded you of the color scheme you want for redecorating? Or did the seeming sound of ocean waves bring you to the beach for your next vacation? Even if you are not able to trace back the exact associations from the music, chances are that it played some role in propelling, extending, or stimulating your thoughts.

Your ability to evoke visual or sensory imagery in response to auditory stimulation or music is a fascinating and enriching aspect of your mental life. It is a function of past experience, as well as imagination. For example, you hear a friend's voice on the phone and remember her face, or you hear a song and imagine the events that go along with it. The capacity of music to spark your imagination is an indication of your creativity and another way in which music affects your mental processes.

The mental imagery and associations evoked by music listening are an important part of your personal connection to music. Even though you may share a musical moment with another person, you develop your own mental, physical, spiritual, and emotional response or association to music listening. Although you may tell someone about your thoughts or feelings in response to music, the actual experience is yours alone, making music is a highly personal event.

Recently the popularity of rock videos has caused some controversy over the personal nature of the imagery and associations evoked by music. Because videos present a visual image, the listener is immediately presented with a context for the music, unlike most other listening experiences. Some people find this disturbing, among them one who writes: "Rock videos threaten to rob us of the special images we conjure up to go with a song [and provide instead] wholesale substitution of common, shared memories for individual memories."[5] Whether or not one agrees with this view, it is clear that rock videos are based on the fact that music does produce imagery powerful enough to be filmed and produced for mass audiences. Hopefully, this new music medium will not interfere with your individual ability to create imagery, thought, association, and memories in response to music listening.

Related to the evocation of mental imagery while listening to music is the connection between music experiences and creativity. As described in Chapter 6, music is a rich source for developing your creativity. Essentially, a creative approach to life implies inventive problem-solving, a wealth of innovative ideas, and a rich supply of resources for managing your personal and professional life. Since each involves mental processes, it is clear to see how mind and creativity go hand in hand.

Music listening that inspires, invites, activates, and stimulates creative thought, as in the evocation of mental imagery, enhances your mind. Once this cycle of thought and creativity is begun, the possibilities for implementing creative action in your life are endless. An example of the power of music listening for developing creativity in work is found in the words of fashion designer Stephen Sprouse: "Rock is the most inspirational thing to me. Hearing the music, seeing the kids who go to the concerts. It represents driving energy to me . . . The Stones, Iggy Pop and Billy Idol. They have an edge. I want that edge in my clothes."[6] Thus, the listening exercise described earlier on pages 183–84 may offer you not only a pleasurable mental journey but also a way in which to develop your mind's potential for creative action in order to enhance your life at home and at work.

• Listen While You Work

It is quite common to hear people say that music helps them think, concentrate, or get their work done. Researchers who have looked into the effects of music listening have validated many of these claims. In two studies, stimulative and sedative music were examined for their impact on the anxiety, concentration, and performance of college students. It was found that listening to stimulative music while taking a test significantly increased the students' concern about their test performance, caused nervousness, tension, and uneasiness, and at times interfered with their concentration. However, sedative music *did not* increase or decrease concern or tension, or interfere with concentration. Despite these seemingly negative findings regarding stimulative music, the authors suggest that such music has the potential to produce positive states of cognitive arousal, such as "increased alertness, activation, participation and attentiveness."[7] In other words, increased activation as a result of stimulative music may at times be positively channeled into increased study and concentration. Perhaps this is why some people actually prefer to study to loud, rather than soft, music.

That there are benefits of music listening during cognitive activities has been supported by other studies as well. According to one, extremely anxious college students achieved higher scores when they listened to background music during test-taking.[8] Another found that scores on a creativity task increased when participants listened to background music.[9] Students in a third study consistently chose to hear music in the background, even when given the option of no music.[10]

In addition to improving performance and concentration, music can also have a positive impact on the acquisition of math, reading, and other language skills in children. Music experiences in these studies included choir, band, music appreciation, beginning instruments, and the use of music in academic instruction through number songs, word songs, and so forth. According to one researcher: "Arts instruction such as music has been found to have a positive effect on basic language development and reading readiness, fosters positive attitudes toward school and the general curriculum and positively influences social and intellectual development and personal adjustment."[11] In accordance with these studies, music therapists have long reported on the positive results attained by incorporating music into curricula for the learning disabled, mentally retarded, and otherwise handicapped children.[12]

Music often positively affects the learning of specific skills or the ability to concentrate because it is a gratifying and pleasurable influence and acts as a positive reinforcer during learning situations. In some instances, direct parallels may be drawn between music and a specific skill. For example, auditory discrimination—the ability to distinguish one sound from another—is basic to spelling, reading, and other language arts. A basic component of auditory discrimination is pitch discrimination, which is the ability to distinguish one tone from another. Music participation, through listening, singing, or playing, involves pitch discrimination, which then enhances auditory-discrimination skills and thus results in improved language skills.[13]

The ideas we have just discussed may give you many clues as to why you have always naturally turned on the radio when it was time to study, or used music as background for solving a problem or providing the necessary inspiration for a creative challenge. Finding the right way to use music for your mind will involve some experimentation with different kinds of music during different mental activities. An easy way to begin is by listening to the radio and to records and tapes from your personal collection while you are engaged in a thinking activity. See what music best inspires your thoughts or helps you through a difficult problem-solving activity. If your thoughts become stuck, try taking a break and listening to some music. Program music, such as the pieces by Tchaikovsky and Vivaldi mentioned earlier, may evoke mental imagery, giving your mind a refreshing break from the task at hand, as well as some ideas to begin anew. The music of Bach may also provide fertile listening for thinking through a project or taking a break while new thoughts emerge. While listening to Bach, pay attention to the intricacies of the melody lines as they intertwine through various themes and variations, similar to the flow of your own thoughts during creative problem-solving activity.

In your search for music to think by, you may find that some music is good to read by, and some too distracting. Music with words, for instance, may bother you when you're really into a book, but it might be just right for thumbing through a magazine on a lazy afternoon. Or you may find that stimulating music helps you balance your checkbook, while relaxing music helps you study for a test. Finally, you may find that the best way to use music for your mind is not to think at all while listening to it. Just as your body needs a rest from physical exertion, so does your mind need a rest from thinking. Music listening may be just the thing to take your mind off the "business at hand" and send it on a peaceful and relaxing journey so that you may return refreshed, ready to think once again. In fact, a significant number of the people we surveyed told us they listen to music when they get home from work to take their minds off the anxieties and concerns of the day. Music for mental relaxation is just as important as music for mental activation.

Whatever your particular preference, let yourself explore music as an accompaniment to or distraction from your mental activities. Use music to enhance your mind. Continue to open your mind to the thoughts, ideas, associations, and memories evoked by music listening. Pay attention to the interaction between your mind and music. Remember . . . music listening is another gateway to a fruitful and creative mental life.

17
Sound and Spirit: Music for the Inner Self

The connection between music and spirituality begins with the very origin of music itself. There is music in almost all religious ritual or ceremony, and the history of music tells us that from the earliest times, music was an inseparable part of religious ceremonies.[1] Nearly all religions and mythologies speak of sound as being divine in nature, and include sound in explanations about the creation of the universe.

The Egyptians "believed that the god Thot . . . created the world not by thought or action but by his voice alone. From his mouth and the sounds it produced four other gods [were] born, who were endowed with similar power and who . . . then peopled and organized the world." Persian and Hindu conceptions of the origins of the universe state that the "world is supposed to have been created by an initial sound which when it emerged from the primordial abyss became light, and little by little part of this light became matter."[2] Another writer describes the divine nature of sound as depicted in the Bible:

> In the beginning was the word, and the word was God. The Word was whistled through the reeds, sung through the trees, and swirled through the chasms of space. In imitation of this sound man formed the vowels and, according to the Kabala, therein is found the name of God. The readings indicate that there is power in the vowels to awaken corresponding spiritual centers in man.[3]

Other references to the spiritual nature of music are found throughout the Old Testament, including the story of David's cure of

King Saul through the music of his harp and the toppling of the walls of Jericho from trumpet blasts.

Although the relationship between music and spirituality is pervasive in religious writings, the spiritual effects of music are perhaps the least understood of all the effects of music. Much of this has to do with the highly personal nature of spirituality and religion. Spirituality, unlike blood pressure or pulse, is not a measurable response to music. Thus, much of what we can know about the effects of music on the spirit comes from various religious writings and personal accounts of spiritual experiences while listening to or playing music. A continuous theme in these sources is the similarity between music and religion as paths to peace, purification, harmony, wisdom, guidance, truth, and healing.

In ancient times, and in many cultures through the ages, music was believed to have magical powers that could "heal sickness, purify the mind and body, and work miracles in the realm of nature."[4] These were the same powers believed to be possessed by the spirits or gods and sought through the practice of religion. Sickness was often thought to be the result of "bad" spirits, and the power of sound and song was used as an intermediary between the person and the spirit in order to effect a cure. These practices solidified the early connection between religion, spirituality, and music, since the individuals called upon to use music for healing were shamans, priests, or other religious figures of the community.[5]

Other early beliefs about the relationship between music, the spirits, and healing are clear from writings of the Greeks, who named Apollo the god of music as well as of medicine. In fact, Greek history is our best source of information for early ideas regarding music and spirituality. As Donald Grout writes:

The word music had a much wider meaning to the Greeks than it has to us. . . . [Among] the Greeks music was thought of as something common or basic to activities that were concerned with truth or beauty. In the teachings of Pythagoras . . . music and arithmetic were not separate; as the understanding of numbers was thought to be the key to the understanding of the whole spiritual and physical universe, so the system of musical sounds and rhythms, being ordered by numbers, was conceived as exemplifying the harmony of the cosmos and corresponding to it.[6]

religion possess is to draw people together. . . . In nearly all cultures, music and religion go hand in hand as a defense against fear and aloneness."[13]

Some of the clearest examples of the combined use of music and religion to provide comfort and community during adversity are found in the spirituals created by enslaved blacks. Through shared song, they continually expressed their faith in God and belief in the power of their prayers, as demonstrated in the following lyrics:

> Oh Freedom! Oh Freedom!
> Oh Freedom, I love thee!
> And before I'll be a slave,
> I'll be buried in my grave,
> And go home to my Lord and be free.[14]

Like religion, music provides a tremendous sense of sharing and unity during times of joy and happiness. Songs that praise God, beauty, and the universe are examples of music used for celebration and exaltation during marriages, births, religious holidays, and other joyous times.

Music for Your Spirit

To some, music as part of spiritual or religious practices is natural. To others, it is an unexplored path. If this is the case for you, there are several ways to begin discovering the spiritual joys of music.

One way is to take the time to listen to religious music, whether your own faith or another's, during holiday times or weekly services. Another is to listen to various forms of folk or ethnic music, which often express a religious or spiritual feeling. Recordings of religious music are easy to find in most record stores and are a way for you to explore the spiritual effects of music in the privacy of your home.

Because spirituality is so personal, it is difficult to suggest the music that would be right for you. You might start by listening to the classics of Eastern and Western spiritual music—Handel's *Messiah*, Bach's B-minor Mass, Gregorian chants, or the Indian ragas recorded by Ravi Shankar. In addition, many recordings

In addition, just as religion teaches proper ethics and morals as the path to good character, so too the Greeks believed in the power of music to create the "right kind of person." Thus, the Greeks developed their systems of music in order to effect the development of appropriate ethics, character, and will. Greek scales were based on mathematical proportion and other natural phenomena, creating an intricate link between man's behavior, music, and the universe.

According to the Greeks, music and musical instruments were a gift from the gods. In return, music was used to address and appease the gods, in the hope that they would hear the music and respond favorably. This is evidence of one of the first known uses of music for personal communication with a deity and is clearly at the root of musical prayer, even as we know it today.

Greek philosophy continued to be incorporated into ideas about music and religion even in the early days of the Christian Church. Churchmen maintained that "all pleasures must be judged in accordance with the Platonic principle that beautiful things exist to remind us of divine and perfect beauty."[7] Music was thus deemed to be the servant of religion, because of its power to uplift the soul to the contemplation of divine things. In fact, until the Renaissance, the Church imposed a virtual ban on any music that was not directly related to religious practice.

References to music as related to or representative of the divine are an integral part of spiritual beliefs about music, particularly apparent in the Eastern religions. As Sufi Inayat Khan writes:

> . . . the art of music has been specially considered divine, because it is the exact miniature of the law working through the whole universe. For instance, if we study ourselves we shall find that the beats of the pulse and the heart, the inhaling and exhaling of the breath, are all the work of rhythm. Life depends on the rhythmic working of the whole mechanism of the body. Breath manifests as voice, as word, as sound; and the sound is continually audible, the sound without and the sound within ourselves. That is music.[8]

Once again we see the link between music, behavior, and the natural universe. In fact, the similarity between music and nature is at the core of beliefs about the spiritual meaning of music. Sufi Inayat Khan continues:

. . . what appeals to us in being near to nature is nature's music. . . . It gives us a sense of exaltation to be moving about in the woods, and to be looking at the green, to be standing near the running water, which has its rhythm, its tone and its harmony. The swinging of the branches in the forest, the rising and falling of the waves, all has its music, and once we contemplate and become one with nature, our hearts open to its music. . . . Something in us has been touched by the rhythmic movement, by the perfect harmony which is so seldom found in this artificial life of ours; it lifts one up and makes one feel that nature is the real temple, the true religion. One moment standing in the midst of nature with open heart is a whole lifetime if one is in tune with nature.[9]

The appeal of music to the heart is also at the core of spirituality and music. Dane Rudhyar, writing on Hindu music, states that "we hear sounds with our ears; we read musical scores with our eyes; we experience tones with our heart."[10] A "heartfelt" response is a frequently reported effect of religious or spiritual music, and something you have probably experienced during holidays or other religious occasions. Whether it be listening to hymns, participating in a gospel choir, learning traditional folk music, or reciting the Sabbath prayer, it is the mixture of emotions, ethnic heritage, and group participation that creates the indescribable joy and feelings of piety during these experiences. People often feel that their heart, spirit, or core has been touched in a unique way. The experience of lifting one's voice in song to God and in unison with others often produces a sense of oneness or wholeness within oneself and with the world and a true perception of the harmony of the spheres as described by the early Greeks.

In many ways, deep spiritual and religious experiences born of music listening are akin to peak experiences. Both kinds of experience may result in a sense of understanding and connection to the universe, renewed values as to the meaning of life, feelings of joyousness, and new perceptions of truth and beauty. Any of these feelings may occur as a result of prayer with music, listening to music while in states of deep relaxation, or performing vocal or instrumental music of any kind. A spiritual experience with music does not necessarily imply that the music or occasion involve a specific religious practice or affiliation. To many, the experience of music is spiritual in and of itself.

Even though we know that music can produce prof[ound] effects, few, if any, explanations exist as to how th[ey] some instances, spiritual or religious feelings towa[rd] learned responses. We feel spiritually moved by mu[sic] times because of our past experiences and associat[ions] rituals and music.

Another explanation for the spiritual effects of [music] the concept of vibration. According to the Sufis, "[...] the root of the whole of creation."[11] Vibration is [...] of all musical sound, whether it be the vibration [...] of a guitar or the vocal chords during singing. Re[cent] the science of physics have demonstrated that we [...] stantly vibrating field of energy, as are all the ani[nate] mate objects of our environment. Our vibrations a[re in] state of interaction and resonance with the other vi[brations] us. Thus, when people say "She has good vibrati[ons" or "I] like the vibrations in here," they are responding [on some] level to the fields of vibration around them, som[etimes] and sometimes not.

Spiritual teachers from Eastern religions teach [that one of the] important paths to spiritual growth involves be[coming attuned] and centered with your own vibration in order t[o be able to tune] in to and become a part of the vibration of th[e universe.] you achieve a sense of your vibration in conce[rt with others,] a deep sense of oneness with and connection [to all of] life usually results. Many believe that the voice [is central] to this form of spiritual growth. Chanting du[ring meditation is] rooted in the belief that the vibrations of the [voice] are powerful in bringing about spiritual harmony [and] resonate within the self and into the outer w[orld.] the voice is considered a prime means of achie[ving] listening to music or playing an instrument a[re ways of using] vibration and sound so as to center oneself [and tune in to] the vibrations of the world. Among the Sufis [a form of spiritual] development called "suma" involves listening [to music as a means] of achieving inner peace and balance in the [...]

People have traditionally turned to music [...] in times of sorrow, distress, and joy. Music [...] comfort, respite, nurturance, support, and co[...] cording to E. Thayer Gaston, "the great val[ue]

in the genre of "new-age" music are geared toward spiritual growth. Look for recordings by Georgia Kelly, William Ackerman, and George Winston. Also, ask your local record-store owner for help in locating old classics and new frontiers of spiritual music. In addition to listening to music, singing or playing music with others can also be the beginning of spiritual experiences with music for you.

As you have been reading along, you probably remembered times when you felt particularly touched by music during a religious ceremony, deep affection for a fellow singer, or a renewed sense of beauty while listening to a favorite symphony. These past experiences may point the ways for you to bring the spiritual effects of music listening into your life.

The goal of spirituality, regardless of religious doctrine, is inner peace, wisdom, and a sense of the truth and beauty of all life. Music is one means by which to achieve this heightened consciousness. Through listening to music, you can continue on your journey toward inner peace and recognition of the essence of life.

• Music for All of You

In the last four chapters we have looked into the effects of music listening on four very important parts of you—your mind, body, spirit, and emotions. Together, these parts make up the wholeness that is you. Although we have examined each part in isolation, in reality they are deeply connected in your being. As physicians, psychotherapists, and researchers are discovering, there is a significant interrelationship between all the different aspects of yourself. Your mind can affect the health of your body, how you think can change how you feel, exercising your body can affect your emotions, and spiritual values can influence your entire approach to life. It makes sense, then, that a major goal of spiritual growth is the integration of all the parts of the self into a whole, centered, and harmonious being.

Changes you make in one part of yourself with music will most likely have an impact on the other parts of yourself. Using music to motivate exercise may result in an improved physical condition, which may then result in greater self-esteem, leading to improved communication with others at work. Or, using music for meditation may result in greater relaxation, leading to improved work skills.

Thus, work in one area will cause a "ripple effect" that will spread through your whole being.

Many of you may find that you are more interested in using music listening for one aspect of yourself than another. Some people are attracted to the physical qualities of music and thus enjoy dancing or exercising to music, rather than listening quietly in a concert hall. Others might be more interested in the form and orchestration of a piece than in the emotion it communicates. A way for you to find your preferred area of access to music is to think back to which of the four chapters you were most interested in reading. If you found yourself skipping through the section on physical effects but avidly reading the one on emotional effects, you have a pretty good clue to where your connection to music lies. Your preferred area of access to music is probably similar to your other preferred modes of interaction in life. Some of us are primarily thinkers, while others are touchers or feelers. When a life problem arises, some of us may choose to think first and feel later, while others may go for a workout at the gym and figure out what to do tomorrow.

Whatever your preferred area of access to music, consult the information presented in the last four chapters for ways to use music listening in the development of a whole, integrated, and balanced you. Begin with your preferred area, then gradually incorporate ideas from each of the other sections into your personalized music program. Similar to the effect of a total body workout, you may be surprised to find that within a few months you've grown throughout your total being. When this occurs, you will have discovered one of the great principles of music and health: The whole is greater than the sum of its parts.

18
Moving Music from the Background to the Foreground

Too often, music functions in the background of our lives. We turn on the radio as we clean our house, hear music in elevators and supermarkets, and absent-mindedly hum commercial jingles. Although background music can serve a beneficial function, as when it motivates us or keeps us company when we are alone, sometimes it can be a cause of concern, as it holds the potential to affect our mind, body, spirit, and emotions in subtle ways without our even knowing it. In fact, music played at low levels in public places is specifically designed to affect you subliminally. Low-level music in medical and dental offices has long been used to calm patients, while music piped into offices, elevators, and supermarkets is often designed with the intention of positively affecting the work habits of employees or encouraging consumer spending. A prime example of this is Muzak. As one writer notes:

> The object of Muzak is not to be really heard, but to serve us as "background" music to relieve stress and give workers or shoppers a lift. In a recent study conducted by Pepperdine University at two supermarkets in Los Angeles, music by Muzak was compared to a "beautiful music" radio station and to a pop-rock station. What the average customer bought was higher on the days Muzak was played.[1]

As music therapists, we believe it is crucial for people to be aware of the music in the background of their lives and its potential influence on their thoughts, feelings, or behavior. Hearing is perhaps the most sensitive of all your senses and the most difficult to shut off to outside stimuli. In the clinical use of music as therapy, this has been a benefit when music was used to reach regressed or uncommunicative individuals. However, the sensitivity of your ears, along with the proven effects of music, demand that your auditory channels be treated with care, consent, and respect.

Your personal preferences for certain types of music will determine to some degree the effects of background music upon you. The research we have discussed in this book clearly indicates that the more you like a piece of music, the greater the positive effects. From this we may assume that the more you dislike a piece of music, the greater the negative effects. Therefore, you deserve personal choice and control over your music and sound environment. Music that is piped into buildings or played when you are put on "hold" on a telephone often denies you the opportunity for personal choice in music listening. Many people experience this music as invasive and bothersome. As one individual has said in response to Muzak, "It's sort of imposing someone else's idea of how you should relax," while another said, "I resent listening to music that's not my own choice."[2]

In addition to such complaints about low-level background music, many people are expressing concern over the increasing amounts of sound to which they are being exposed as a result of our technological society. Research on the effects of sound and noise on behavior suggests that "noise may have an adverse effect on emotional well being . . . [and] can reduce both sociability and sensitivity to the needs of others," and that "workers habitually exposed to very high intensity noise show increased incidence of nervous complaints, nausea, headaches, instability, argumentativeness, sexual impotence, mood changes and anxiety."[3] Now added to such sources of discomfort as industrial noises and other harsh sounds created by fast-paced city living is another: loud music. One study suggests that exciting or stimulative music may produce more feelings of anxiety and aggression than calm music or no music at all.[4] Thus, music blasting from radios in public places or from stores wishing to attract your attention adds to the growing amount of noise pollution in your environment and thereby to potential adverse effects upon your health.

At times, what we listen to by choice on the radio is subject to the control of others. Research regarding the role of disc jockeys

in determining listener preferences has shown that repetition increases preference. Therefore, the more we hear something, the
more we tend to like it. Repetition of particular pieces, especially
in the genre of "top-40" tunes, may even influence our record-
buying patterns. Consequently, some important questions about
music in our environment need to be considered:

> What is the function and value of using music in business and
> work areas, marketplaces, airplanes and waiting rooms? What
> are the effects on listeners' behaviors of the various uses of
> music in radio and television commercials, or for television and
> motion picture backgrounds? When do uses become abuses—
> when and how does supermarket music subtly influence purchas-
> ing behavior even though the consumer is not conscious of
> it? When do loud music presentations become physically harm-
> ful? What are the effects of subliminal sound messages scram-
> bled into a normal musical context? And when do campaign
> song commercials and other politically-oriented songs become
> mind-controlling propaganda?[5]

You have the right to control your own music and sound environment. For most of us, most of the time, music is a joyous gift
and source of nurturance and renewal in our lives. Yet, the when,
where, how, and what we listen to must be a matter of personal
choice. Without it, the cacophony of uncontrolled sounds and
music in our world may eventually cause us so much discomfort
as to rule out the possibility of appreciating the true beauty and
purpose of music.

For this reason, we encourage you to move music from the
background to the foreground of your life, and take charge of
the sounds and music you hear. Whenever possible, listen to music
on high-quality equipment, at comfortable volumes, in an environment free from sound distractions. Minimizing distortions or interference in what you hear will maximize the benefits you will receive.

Finally, let yourself also experience the joys of silence. Through
silence, we achieve appreciation of music. In the words of Murray
Schafer:

> Thus, just as man strives for perfection, all sound aspires to
> the condition of silence, to the eternal life of the "Music of
> the Spheres." Can silence be heard? Yes, if we could extend

our consciousness outward to the universe and to eternity, we could hear silence. Through the practice of contemplation, little by little, the muscles and the mind relax and the whole body opens out to become an ear. When the Indian yogi attains a state of liberation from the senses, he hears the anāhata, the "unstruck" sound. Then perfection is achieved. The secret hieroglyph of the universe is revealed. Timbre becomes audible and flows down filling the receiver with tones and light.[6]

V
A Deeper Look at Yourself Through Sound

Thus music has fulfilled its mission
whenever our hearts are satisfied.
—Hans Mersmann

19

Music Therapy

Susan and John come to the music therapy session looking for ways to improve and expand their communication with each other, since they recently found themselves unable to effectively use words to resolve difficulties in their relationship. Through the use of music and sound, they hope to re-establish the close communication and mutual understanding they had previously shared.

To begin their work, Susan and John are asked to improvise some music together. They sit on the floor facing each other, surrounded by drums, small rhythm instruments, xylophones, and other instruments provided by the music therapist. As their music begins, they stare into each other's eyes and watch each other carefully. Their sounds, rhythms, melodies, and harmonies rise, mingle, and dissipate. They each explore the different instruments and sound qualities available to them.

As their improvisation continues, the therapist begins to notice a lack of unity in their music. Although it looks as if they are playing together, their music indicates no rhythmic, melodic or harmonic connection between them. There are no pauses to listen to each other, or any attempts to blend their sounds. After about ten minutes of improvising, Susan picks up a small pair of cymbals. With tears streaming down her face, she moves her two hands together as if to play them, but stops just short of making any sound. As she repeats this action, her frustration and silence exemplify her experience of the absence of hearing or being heard in her relationship with John.

Afterward, a discussion with the therapist about their thoughts, feelings, and actions during the improvisation helps Susan and

John understand how they each contribute to their communication difficulties. Susan has a tendency to express her wants and needs in a way that cannot be heard by John, and hopes instead that he will figure out what they are. John has a tendency to become so involved in his own attempts to communicate that he does not take the time to stop and listen to Susan.

To solidify their understanding of the work and begin a new, more effective pattern of communication, Susan and John begin another improvisation. Already change is apparent as they take the time to listen to each other's music, respond through sound, and create a harmonious integration of their two solos.

In following up a few weeks later, Susan and John tell the therapist that the music therapy work has changed their relationship and opened new paths of communication. The metaphor of the unheard cymbal has lingered as a way to avoid communication breakdown. Susan reports that whenever she begins to feel unheard by John, all she needs to do is lift her hands and re-enact the motion of her silent cymbal.

Like many people each year, Susan and John sought professional help in attempting to resolve personal and interpersonal difficulties. However, they were unusual in their choice of music therapy, for, unlike most people, they were aware of music therapy and the qualified practitioners in their community. By determining to work with a music therapist, they chose to take a deeper look at themselves through sound and music.

Simply defined, music therapy is the prescribed use of music in the treatment and rehabilitation of persons experiencing physical, mental, or emotional disorders.[1] Although many believe music therapy to be a new field, its origins and practices are really quite ancient. References about the use of music in the Bible, as in the story of David and King Saul, or by the Greeks to establish inner harmony are just two examples of the enduring belief in the curative powers of music. Music therapy is, therefore, based on centuries of knowledge and understanding about the inherent healing nature of music.

As a form of therapy, music is extremely effective because we are all innately musical beings. Our earliest perceptions of and communications with ourselves and others occur through sound and rhythm. We hear our cries and know we exist; we are rocked and know the comforting presence of another; our calls are answered and a relationship is formed. As social beings, we strive for balanced harmony with others while maintaining the integrity of our solo. Recognizing and using our musicality provides another access to self-understanding and awareness.

Throughout the ages and into the present, people have sought the comfort of music in times of sorrow and distress, expressed with sound what could not be conveyed by words, experienced community and belonging through shared song, and affirmed their creativity and potential through discovery of personal melodies. Music therapists continue to expand these traditions by offering music experiences that are designed to enhance healthful potential, work through archaic patterns of functioning, and foster positive connections with others. The theory and practice of music therapy is strongly aligned with humanistic traditions in psychotherapy that regard creative expression as primary to the process of achieving health and self-actualization.

Music therapists work with clients on a long-term or short-term basis, either individually or in groups. The music used during therapy sessions may be improvised or already composed and structured, based on the needs of the client(s). In many instances, clients actively participate in the creation of live music, making use of a large assortment of high-quality nonsymphonic instruments specifically designed to provide immediate access to music-making. Therefore, clients do not need prior music training or experience in order to fully benefit from effective treatment.

In addition to playing music, clients may also listen to live or recorded music, move to music, or draw to music, again determined by treatment needs. Some music therapists add other variations to treatment, depending on their professional training, psychotherapy orientation, and client population. For example, the case of Susan and John involved the free use of words in addition to the music-making, owing to the verbal capacities of these clients and the verbal psychotherapy training of the therapist.

The professional development of music therapy began in the 1940s in response to the influx of veterans returning home from World War II. During this time, many professionally trained musicians volunteered to play music for the patients, in order to entertain them and to provide a pleasurable way for them to pass their time. Gradually the musicians began to notice and document other effects the music was having on the patients. Increased social-ization, lifting of depression, emotional release, improved morale, and greater contact with reality were just a few of the gains made by patients regularly exposed to music. As a result, professional training for music therapists was instituted, and graduate and un-dergraduate programs were in full swing by the 1950s. A growing body of research, theory and methodology supported the clinical use of music.

Today, two national associations, the American Association for Music Therapy and the National Association for Music Therapy, continue to advance the professional development of music ther-apy in the United States through their approval of university train-ing programs, certification of qualified individuals, support of research, and education of health-care and legislative groups as to the benefits of music therapy. There are presently seventy-six music-therapy programs in the United States, ranging from the B.A. to the Ph.D level, and approximately 2,000 practicing music therapists. In addition, at least thirty-four international associations and/or training programs currently exist throughout the world.

The increasing acceptance and growth of music therapy as an effective treatment is evidenced by the fact that music therapists are presently found working with every imaginable client popula-tion, in just about any type of treatment facility. Traditionally, music therapy services have been sought as an alternative treatment for clients who were unable to speak or use insight for personal growth, or were otherwise handicapped in their abilities to express themselves. Because music is a form of nonverbal communication, therapists found that they were able to achieve results with clients who had previously been untreatable or unreachable. In this regard, the success of music therapy with autistic children has been most well documented and publicized.[2] In spite of this, music therapists have continued to explore new territory, and work with verbally proficient clients has begun to steadily increase as the awareness of the healing potential of music for *all* people has grown.

Typical music therapy treatment groups have included the men-tally retarded, learning disabled, physically handicapped, emotion-ally disturbed, and geriatric populations. Still the list of individuals serviced by music therapists continues to grow. Cancer patients and other medically ill individuals now benefit from music therapy in many urban hospitals.[3] Recently, significant work has been accomplished even with deaf children[4] and drug and substance abusers.[5] In each of these instances, individuals have experienced the gift of music in aiding their recovery from physical, mental, or emotional distress.

One group that has been consistently overlooked for music-therapy treatment is normal adults in the community, such as Susan and John. Many of these people readily seek the help of psychotherapists in resolving personal and professional difficulties, but are unaware of music therapy and the ways in which it may be used to facilitate growth and to work through problems. Clearly music therapy, like any other therapy, is not the appropriate treatment choice for every kind of problem or every type of person. However, increased public awareness is leading toward the inclusion of music therapy as a primary or adjunctive treatment option in the array of psychotherapies presently available to community members.

Much of the theory and research presented in this book comes from the field of music therapy and our work as music therapists. We have used this information to introduce you to the potential of music as a healthful and nourishing source for inner growth and awareness. Although we believe there is a place for music in everyone's life and that people can grow and gain through music experiences, there are times when the guidance of a qualified music therapist is indicated. We do not believe in the use of music for therapy by untrained persons or for self-treatment of serious emotional or physical problems. Emotional distress, severe physical tension or illness, relationship difficulties, or work-related problems that interfere with one's ability to function in an effective manner usually call for professional help.

At times when a deeper look into your life is necessary in order to grow and change, music therapy might be a valuable investment in your life and happiness. Further information about music therapy and how to locate a trained music therapist in your area may be obtained by contacting a professional music therapy association. Names and addresses of such associations are listed in the Appendix. Although we strongly encourage you to use this book as a guide to greater fulfillment and personal growth through music, we also encourage you to seek professional guidance when necessary. The benefits of exploring yourself through sound await you!

A Final Note

Music is not just a special part of life; it represents life itself. From it we receive inspiration, excitement, and emotional enrichment. With it we create, communicate, and express who we are.

In the wake of music comes growth and energy that can facilitate important change. Even one song can make a difference in your life. Because involvement in music is natural and healthy, when we choose to listen, sing, or play, we choose to grow. Abraham Maslow describes this process succinctly: ". . . anything that would help the person to move in the direction of greater psychological health or fuller humanness would amount to changing the whole person."[1] With each musical step you take, whether it be listening closely to a special song, singing a new tune, or mastering an instrumental passage, comes movement and growth of your entire being. Each musical step is a microcosm of the whole person's choice for health.

Although a learning process can help you become more musically and technically adept as a musician, you needn't take a single lesson to truly appreciate music or to know what it really is. You need only listen to yourself. The music is within you, as it has existed in all people since the beginning of time. Your song, your sounds, and your rhythms reflect your unique nature.

These gifts are so native to us that we tend to forget they are there. With your new knowledge of the magic that music holds for you, let yourself know your song and its meanings. Open your ears to the sounds around you, and your heart to the sounds of others. A vibrant, joyous life awaits you as you release your music into the world and celebrate the beauty of the natural musician you are.

Appendix
Music Therapy
Associations in
North America

AMERICAN ASSOCIATION FOR MUSIC THERAPY
66 Morris Avenue
Springfield, New Jersey   07081
201-379-1100

CANADIAN ASSOCIATION FOR MUSIC THERAPY
P.O. Box 1208
Woodstock, Ontario
N4S 8T6 Canada

NATIONAL ASSOCIATION FOR MUSIC THERAPY
1133 Fifteenth Street N.W.
Suite 1000
Washington, D.C.   20005
202-429-9440

For a complete listing of names and addresses of other music therapy associations throughout the world, contact the American Association for Music Therapy for their publication *International Newsletter of Music Therapy,* No. 2, 1984. ($4 per copy)

Footnotes

1: The Natural Role of Music in Your Life

1. Verny, T., and Kelly, J., *The Secret Life of the Unborn Child* (New York: Delta Books, 1981). See also Lewis, P., "What's on Babies' Minds When They Come into the World?" *The New York Times,* August 26, 1984.
2. Byrne, J. M., and Horowitz, F. D., "Rocking as a Soothing Intervention: The Influence of Direction and Type of Movement," *Infant Behavior and Development* 4 (1981).
3. Salk, L., "The Effects of the Normal Heartbeat Sound on the Behavior of the Newborn Infant: Implications for Mental Health," *World Mental Health* 12 (1960): 168–75.
4. Brown, C., "Reactions of Infants to Their Parents' Voices," *Infant Behavior and Development* 2 (1979).
5. Mills, M., and Melhuish, E., "Recognition of Mother's Voice in Early Infancy," *Science* 252 (1974).
6. Ostwald, P., *The Semiotics of Human Sound* (The Hague: Mouton & Co. N.V., 1973), 54.
7. Ibid., 39.
8. Ibid., 203.
9. Spitz, R., "Hospitalism: An Inquiry into the Genesis of Psychiatric Conditions in Early Childhood," *Psychoanalytic Studies of the Child* 1 (1945).
10. Berne, E., *Games People Play* (New York: Ballantine Books, 1964), 13.

2: Living Rhythms

1. Meerloo, J., *Unobtrusive Communication* (Assen, Netherlands: Van

3. Kestenberg, J., "The Role of Movement Patterns in Development," *Psychoanalytic Quarterly* (January 1965): 31.
4. Ibid.
5. Condon, W. S., "Neonate Movement Is Synchronized with Adult Speech: Interactional Participation and Language Acquisition," *Science* 183 (1974): 99–101.
6. Ibid.

3: Your Song in the World

1. Boyd, S., "Developmental Processes in the Child's Acquisition of Syntax," in Cohen, S., and Comiskey, T., *Child Development* (Illinois: F. E. Peacock, Inc., 1977).
2. Ibid.
3. Ostwald, P., "Musical Behavior in Early Childhood," *Developmental Medicine and Child Neurology* 15 (1973): 367.
4. Ibid.
5. McDonald, M., "Transitional Tunes and Musical Development," *Psychoanalytic Studies of the Child* 25 (1970).

4: The Harmony of Life

1. Alvin, J., *Music Therapy* (New York: Basic Books, 1975), 39.

5: You Need Music!

1. Cage, J., in Hill, S., and Turner, A., *The Hearts of Space Guide to Cosmic, Transcendent and Inner Space Music* (San Francisco: Music from the Hearts of Space, 1981), 48.

6: Develop Your Creativity with Music

1. Maslow, A. H., *The Farther Reaches of Human Nature* (New York: Penguin Books, 1971), 79, 96.
2. May, R., *The Courage to Create* (New York: Bantam Books, 1975), viii.
3. Arietti, S., *Creativity: The Magic Synthesis* (New York: Basic Books, 1976), 4, 10.
4. Doerschuk, B., "The Crisis in Music Education: Classical Virtuoso Lorin Hollander Offers a Diagnosis & a Ray of Hope," *Keyboard* 10:4 (1984): 20.
5. Hanschumaker, J., "The Effects of Arts Education on Intellectual and Social Development: A Review of Selected Literature," *Council for Research in Music Education Bulletin* 61 (Winter 1980): 24.

6. Ibid., 18.
7. McNiff, S., *The Arts and Psychotherapy* (Springfield, Il.: Charles C. Thomas, 1981), 54.
8. Cousins, N., *Anatomy of an Illness as Perceived by the Patient* (New York: Bantam Books, 1979), 72–73.
9. Ibid., 74.

7: Discover Joy Through Music

1. Maslow, A. H., *The Farther Reaches of Human Nature* (New York: Penguin Books, 1971), 172.
2. Steiner, C., *Scripts People Live* (New York: Bantam Books, 1974), 173.
3. Copland, A., *Music and Imagination* (Cambridge, Mass.: Harvard University Press, 1980), 17.
4. Maslow, note 1, 169.
5. Ibid., 170–71.

8: Music for Greater Self-Esteem

1. Maslow, A. H., *The Farther Reaches of Human Nature* (New York: Penguin Books, 1971), 32.
2. Ostwald, P., *The Semiotics of Human Sound* (The Hague: Mouton & Co. N.V., 1973), 66.
3. Ibid., 39.
4. Ibid., 61.

9: Building Confidence with Music

1. Perls, F., Hefferlino, R., and Goodman, P., *Gestalt Therapy* (New York: Bantam Books, 1951), 77.
2. Ibid., 76–77.
3. Bernstein, S., *With Your Own Two Hands: Self-Discovery Through Music.* (New York: Schirmer Books, Macmillan, 1981), 9–10.

10: Music for Closer Communication

1. Gaston, E. T., *Music in Therapy* (New York: Macmillan, 1968), 23.
2. Epperson, G., "Thought and Feeling in Musical Expression," *The American Music Teacher* 32:2 (1982): 43.
3. Langer, S. K., *Philosophy in a New Key: A Study in the Symbolism of Reason, Rite and Art* (Cambridge, Mass.: Harvard University Press, 1980), 226–28.
4. Reese, S., "Forms of Feeling: The Aesthetic Theory of Susanne K. Langer," *Music Educator's Journal* (1977): 46.

5. Polster, E., and Polster, M., *Gestalt Therapy Integrated* (New York: Vintage Books, Random House, 1973), 103.

11: Playing an Instrument

1. Gibbons, A. C., "Music Aptitude Profile Scores in a Noninstitutionalized Elderly Population," *Journal of Research in Music Education* 3:1 (1982): 28.
2. Steiner, C., *Scripts People Live* (New York: Bantam Books, 1974), 191–92.
3. Maslow, A. H., "Some Differences Between Intrinsic and Extrinsic Learning," in Hamacheck, D. E., ed., *Human Dynamics in Psychology and Education* (Boston: Allyn and Bacon, 1968).
4. Robbins, C., Unpublished lecture, New York University, July 2, 1979.
5. Wilson, F. R., "Mind, Muscle and Music," *The American Music Teacher* 32:1 (1982): 14.
6. Ibid.: 14–15.
7. Wolff, E., Personal communication, May 8, 1984.
8. Kemp, A. E., "Personality Differences Between the Players of String, Woodwind, Brass and Keyboard Instruments, and Singers," *Council for Research in Music Education Bulletin* 66–67 (Spring–Summer 1981): 33–36.
9. Ostwald, P., *The Semiotics of Human Sound* (The Hague: Mouton & Co. N.V., 1973), 186–87.
10. Schmaltz, J., "Sound of Avant-Garde Fills Hartford Streets," *The New York Times,* July 7, 1984.

12: Singing Your Heart Out

1. Moses, P., *The Voice of Neurosis* (New York: Grune & Stratton, 1954), 17.
2. Lowen, A., *Bioenergetics* (New York: Penguin Books, 1975), 270.
3. Sokolov, L., Personal communication, July 17, 1984.
4. Keyes, L. E., *Toning: The Creative Power of the Voice* (California: DeVorss and Co., 1973), 12–13.
5. Hodges, D. A., ed., *Handbook of Music Psychology* (Kansas: National Association for Music Therapy, 1980), 149.
6. Reich, W., *The Function of the Orgasm* (New York: Touchstone, Simon & Schuster, 1973) 307–09.
7. Ibid., 300–01.
8. Sokolov, note 3.
9. Ibid.
10. Lowen, note 2.
11. Ibid., 271.

13: Listen to What You Hear

1. Merriam, A. P., *The Anthropology of Music* (Chicago: Northwestern University Press, 1964), 111.
2. Gaston, E. T., in Hodges, D. A., ed., *Handbook of Music Psychology* (Kansas: National Association for Music Therapy, 1980), 393.
3. Ibid., 126.
4. Ibid., 121.
5. Ibid., 122.
6. Ibid., 124.
7. Ibid., 131–32.
8. Chenoweth, L., "The Rhetoric of Hope and Despair: A Study of the Jimi Hendrix Experience and the Jefferson Airplane," *American Quarterly* 23 (Spring 1971): 25–45.

14: Let's Get Physical! Music for the Body

1. Dainow, E., "Physical Effects and Motor Responses to Music," *Journal of Research in Music Education* 25 (1977): 212–13.
2. Hodges, D. A., ed., *Handbook of Music Psychology* (Kansas: National Association for Music Therapy, 1980), 393.
3. Bonny, H. L., "Music Listening for Intensive Coronary Care Units: A Pilot Project," *Music Therapy: The Journal of the American Association for Music Therapy* 3:1 (1983): 11.
4. Hodges, note 2, 394.
5. Bonny, note 3, 11.
6. Hodges, note 2, 142.
7. Kibler, V. E., and Rider, M. S., "Effects of Progressive Muscle Relaxation and Music on Stress as Measured by Finger Temperature Response," *Journal of Clinical Psychology* 39:2 (March 1983): 213–15.
8. Pearce, K. A., "Effects of Different Types of Music on Physical Strength," *Perceptual and Motor Skills* 53 (1981): 351–52.
9. Hanser, S. B., Larson, S. C., and O'Connell, A. S., "The Effect of Music on Relaxation of Expectant Mothers During Labor," *Journal of Music Therapy* 20:2 (1983): 50–58. See also Gardner, W. J., Licklider, J. C., and Weisz, A. A., "Suppression of Pain by Sound," *Science* 132 (1960): 32–33.
10. Bonny, note 3, 14. See also Wallis, C., "Unlocking Pain's Secrets," *Time* (June 11, 1984): 66.
11. Bonny, H. L., *Music Rx: A Hospital Music Program* (ICM West: P.O. Box 173, Port Townsend, Wash. 98368, 1984), 4.

12. Wolfe, D. E., "Pain Rehabilitation and Music Therapy," *Journal of Music Therapy* 15:4 (1978): 176.
13. Brody, R., "Music Medicine," *Omni* (April 1984): 24.
14. Hanser et. al., note 9. See also Clark, M. E., McCorkle, R. R., and Williams, S. B., "Music Therapy Assisted Labor and Delivery," *Journal of Music Therapy* 18:2 (1981): 88–100.
15. Ibid.: 57.
16. MacClelland, D. C., "Music in the Operating Room," *Association of Operating Nurses Journal* 29 (1979): 252–60.
17. Trotter, R. J., "Maybe It's the Music," *Psychology Today* (May 1984): 8.

15: What A Feeling! Music for the Emotions

1. Merriam, A. P., *The Anthropology of Music* (Chicago: Northwestern University Press, 1964), 219.
2. WPIX-FM Radio, New York City, N.Y.
3. Langer, S. K., *Philosophy in a New Key* (Cambridge, Mass.: Harvard University Press, 1980), 226–28.
4. Hodges, D. A., ed., *Handbook of Music Psychology* (Kansas: National Association for Music Therapy, 1980), 202–03.
5. Ibid., 143.
6. Bonny, H. L., and Savary, L., *Music and Your Mind* (New York: Harper and Row, 1973), 161. See also Hevner, K., "An Experimental Study of the Affective Value of Sounds and Poetry," *American Journal of Psychology* 49 (1937): 419–34.
7. Ibid., Table I.
8. Greenberg, R. P., and Fisher, S., "Selective Effects upon Women of Exciting and Calm Music," *Perceptual and Motor Skills* 34 (1972): 987–90.
9. Smith, C. A., and Morris, L. W., "Effects of Stimulative and Sedative Music on Cognitive and Emotional Components of Anxiety," *Psychological Reports* 38 (1976): 1187. See also Smith, C. A., and Morris, L. W., "Differential Effects of Stimulative and Sedative Music on Anxiety, Concentration and Performance," *Psychological Reports* 41 (1977): 1047.
10. Hodges, note 4, 149. See also Shatin, L., "Alteration of Mood via Music: A Study of the Vectoring Effect," *Journal of Psychology* 75 (1970): 81–86.

16: Mind over Music: Music to Think By

1. Hodges, D. A., ed., *Handbook of Music Psychology* (Kansas: National Association for Music Therapy, 1980), 143.

2. Marks, L. E., "Synesthesia: The Lucky People with Mixed-Up Senses," *Psychology Today* (June 1975): 51.
3. Bookspan, M., *101 Masterpieces of Music and Their Composers* (New York: Dolphin Books, 1973).
4. Bonny, H. L., and Savar, L., *Music and Your Mind* (New York: Harper & Row, 1973), 17.
5. Zorn, E., "Memories Aren't Made of This," *Newsweek* (February 13, 1984): 16.
6. Duka, J., "The Rock Connection," *The New York Times (Fashions of the Times),* August 26, 1984.
7. Smith, C. A., and Morris, L. W., "Effects of Stimulative and Sedative Music on Cognitive and Emotional Components of Anxiety," *Psychological Reports* 38 (1976): 1187–93.
8. Stanton, H. E., "The Effect of Music on Test Anxiety," *Australian Psychologist* 8 (1973): 220–28.
9. Kaltsonis, B., "Effect of Sound on Creative Performance," *Psychological Reports* 33 (1973): 737–38.
10. Sanders, S. J., Tedford, W. H., and Hardy, B. W., "Effects of Musical Stimuli on Creativity," *Psychological Record* 2 (1977): 463–71.
11. Hanschumaker, J., "The Effects of Arts Education on Intellectual and Social Development: A Review of Selected Literature," *Council for Research in Music Education Bulletin* 61 (Winter 1980): 10–25.
12. Graham, R. M., *Music for the Exceptional Child* (Reston, Va.: Music Educators National Conference, 1975).
13. McMahon, O., "The Relationship of Music Discrimination Training to Reading and Associated Auditory Skills," *Council for Research in Music Education Bulletin* 59 (Summer 1979): 68.

17: Sound and Spirit: Music for the Inner Self

1. Grout, D. J., *A History of Western Music* (New York: W. W. Norton & Co., 1973), 3.
2. Alvin, J., *Music Therapy* (New York: Basic Books, 1975), 3, 7.
3. Winston, S. R., *Music as the Bridge* (Virginia: A.R.E. Press, 1972), 53.
4. Grout, note 1, 3.
5. McNiff, S., *The Arts in Psychotherapy* (Springfield, Ill.: Charles C. Thomas, 1981), 3.
6. Grout, note 1, 6–7.
7. Ibid., 9.
8. Khan, Sufi Inayat, *Music* (New York: Samuel Weiser, Inc., 1977), 2–3.
9. Ibid., 9–10.

10. Rudyar, D., *The Rebirth of Hindu Music* (New York: Samuel Weiser, Inc., 1979), 28.
11. Khan, note 8, 21.
12. Ibid., 25.
13. Gaston, E. T., *Music in Therapy* (New York: MacMillan, 1968), 23.
14. Cone, J. H., *The Spirituals and the Blues* (New York: The Seabury Press, 1972), 30.

18: Moving Music from the Background to the Foreground

1. Barclay, D., "Muzak Survives the Critics and Celebrates Its 50th Birthday," *The Citizen Register,* July 22, 1984.
2. Ibid.
3. Cohen, S., "Sound Effects on Behavior," *Psychology Today* (October 1981): 38, 42.
4. Greenberg, R. P., and Fisher, S., "Selective Effects upon Women of Exciting and Calm Music," *Perceptual and Motor Skills* 34 (1972): 987–90.
5. Hodges, D. A., *Handbook of Music Psychology* (Kansas: National Association for Music Therapy, 1980), 152, 155.
6. Schafer, M., *The Tuning of the World* (New York: Alfred A. Knopf, 1977), 262.

19: Music Therapy

1. Alvin, J., *Music Therapy* (New York: Basic Books, 1975), 4.
2. Nordoff, P., and Robbins, C., *Creative Music Therapy* (New York: John Day, Co., 1977).
3. Brody, B., "Music Medicine," *Omni* (April 1984): 24. See also Wallis, C., "Unlocking Pain's Secrets," *Time* (June 11, 1984): 66.
4. Robbins, C., and Robbins, C., *Music for the Hearing Impaired* (St. Louis: Magnamusic-Baton, 1980).
5. Murphy, M., "Music Therapy: A Self-Help Group Experience for Substance Abuse Patients," *Music Therapy: The Journal of the American Association for Music Therapy* 3:1, (1983): 52–62.

A Final Note

1. Maslow, A. H., *The Farther Reaches of Human Nature* (New York: Penguin Books, 1971), 71.
Quote, p. 13. Langer, S. K., *Philosophy in a New Key. A Study in the Symbolism of Reason, Rite and Art* (Cambridge, Mass.: Harvard University Press, 1980), 244.

Quote, p. 51. Bach, R., *Illusions. The Adventures of a Reluctant Messiah* (New York: Laurel/Eleanor Friede, Dell, 1977), 100.

Quote, p. 109. Hill, S., and Turner, A., *The Hearts of Space Guide to Cosmic, Transcendent, and Innerspace Music* (San Francisco: Music from the Hearts of Space, 1981), 19.

Quote, p. 153. Ibid., 67.

Bibliography

Alvin, Juliette. *Music therapy.* 1975. New York: Basic Books.

Apel, Willi, and Ralph T. Daniel. 1960. *The Harvard brief dictionary of music.* New York: Pocket Books.

Arietti, Silvano. 1976. *Creativity: The magic synthesis.* New York: Basic Books.

Bach, Richard. 1977. *Illusions.* New York: Laurel/Eleanor Friede.

Barclay, Dolores. 1984. Muzak survives the critics and celebrates its 50th birthday. *The Citizen Register* (July 22).

Berne, Eric. 1964. *Games people play.* New York: Ballantine.

Bernstein, Seymour. 1981. *With your own two hands: Self-discovery through music.* New York: Macmillan.

Bonny, Helen L. 1983. Music listening for intensive coronary care units: A pilot project. *Music Therapy: The Journal of the American Association for Music Therapy* 3(1):4–16.

Bonny, Helen L., and Louis Savary. 1973. *Music and your mind.* New York: Harper & Row.

Bonny, Helen L. 1984. *Music Rx: A hospital music program.* ICM West: P.O. Box 173, Port Townsend, Washington, 98368.

Bookspan, Martin. 1973. *101 Masterpieces of music and their composers.* New York: Dolphin.

Brody, Robert. 1984. Music medicine. *Omni* (April):24.

Brown, Cheryl J. 1979. Reaction of infants to their parents' voices. *Infant Behavior and Development* 2:295–300.

Byrne, Joseph M., and Frances D. Horowitz. 1981. Rocking as a soothing intervention: The influence of direction and type of movement. *Infant Behavior and Development* 4:207–18.

Chenoweth, Lawrence. 1971. The rhetoric of hope and despair: A study of the Jimi Hendrix Experience and the Jefferson Airplane. *American Quarterly* (Spring):25–45.

Clark, M. E., R. R. McCorkle, and S. B. Williams. 1981. Music therapy-assisted labor and delivery. *Journal of Music Therapy* 18(2):88–100.

Cohen, Sheldon. 1981. Sound effects on behavior. *Psychology Today* (October):38–45.

Condon, William S. 1974. Neonate movement is synchronized with adult speech: Interactional participation and language acquisition. *Science* 183:99–100.

Cone, James H. 1972. *The spirituals and the blues.* New York: Seabury.

Copland, Aaron. 1980. *Music and imagination.* Cambridge, Mass.: Harvard.

Cousins, Norman. 1981. *Anatomy of an illness as perceived by the patient.* New York: Bantam.

Dainow, Elliot. 1977. Physical effects and motor responses to music. *Journal of Research in Music Education* 25:211–21.

Doerschuk, Bob. 1984. The crisis in music education: classical virtuoso Lorin Hollander offers a diagnosis & a ray of hope. *Keyboard* 10(4):19–26.

Duka, John. 1984. The rock connection. *The New York Times* (August 26).

Epperson, Gordon. 1982. Thought and feeling in musical expression. *The American Music Teacher* 32 (2).

Gardner, W. J., J. C. Licklider, and A. A. Weisz. 1960. Suppression of pain by sound. *Science* 132:32–33.

Gaston, E. Thayer. 1968. *Music in therapy.* New York: Macmillan.

Gibbons, Alicia Clair. 1982. Music aptitude profile scores in a noninstitutionalized elderly population. *Journal of Research in Music Education* 30(1).

Graham, Richard M. 1975. *Music for the exceptional child.* Reston, Va.: Music Educators National Conference.

Greenberg, R. P., and S. Fisher. 1972. Selective effects upon women of exciting and calm music. *Perceptual and Motor Skills* 34:987–90.

Grout, Donald Jay. 1973. *A history of Western music.* New York: W. W. Norton.

Hamel, Peter Michael. 1978. *Through music to the self.* Boulder, Co.: Shambala.

Hanser, S. B., S. C. Larson, and A. S. O'Connell. 1983. The effect of music on relaxation of expectant mothers during labor. *Journal of Music Therapy* 20(2):50–58.

Hanschumaker, James. 1980. The effects of arts education on intellectual and social development: A review of selected literature. *Council for Research in Music Education Bulletin* 61 (Winter).

Hevner, Kate. 1937. An experimental study of the affective value of sounds and poetry. *American Journal of Psychology* 49:419–34.

Hill, Stephen, and Anna Turner. 1981. *The hearts of space guide to cosmic, transcendent and innerspace music.* San Francisco: Music from the Hearts of Space.

Hodges, Donald A., ed. 1980. *Handbook of music psychology.* Kansas: National Association for Music Therapy.

Khan, Sufi Inayat. 1977. *Music.* New York: Samuel Weiser.

Kaltsonis, B. 1973. Effect of sound on creative performance. *Psychological Reports* 33:737–38.

Kemp, Anthony E. 1981. Personality differences between the players of string, woodwind, brass and keyboard instruments, and singers. *Council for Research in Music Education Bulletin* 66–67 (Spring–Summer).

Kestenberg, Judith S. 1965. The role of movement patterns in development. *Psychoanalytic Quarterly* (January):1–35.

Keyes, Laurel Elisabeth. 1973. *Toning: The creative power of the voice.* Calif.: DeVorss.

Kibler, V. E., and M. S. Rider. 1983. Effects of progressive muscle relaxation and music on stress as measured by finger temperature response. *Journal of Clinical Psychology* 39(2) (March):213–15.

Langer, Susanne K. 1980. *Philosophy in a new key.* Cambridge, Mass.: Harvard.

Lewis, Peter. 1984. What's on babies' minds when they come into the world. *The New York Times* (August 26).

Lowen, Alexander. 1975. *Bioenergetics.* New York: Penguin.

MacClelland, D. C. 1979. Music in the operating room. *Association of Operating Nurses Journal* 29:252–60.

McDonald, Marjorie. 1970. Transitional tunes and musical development. *Psychoanalytic Studies of the Child* 25:503.

Marks, Lawrence E. 1975. Synesthesia: The lucky people with mixed-up senses. *Psychology Today* (June):48–52.

Maslow, Abraham H. 1971. *The farther reaches of human nature.* New York: Penguin.

———. 1968. Some differences between intrinsic and extrinsic learning, in D. E. Hamachek, ed. *Human dynamics in psychology and education.* Boston: Allyn and Bacon.

May, Rollo. *The courage to create.* 1975. New York: Bantam.

McNiff, Shawn. 1981. *The arts in psychotherapy.* Springfield, Il.: Charles C. Thomas.

McMahon, Olive. 1979. The relationship of music discrimination training to reading and associated auditory skills. *Council for Research in Music Education Bulletin* 59 (Summer):68.

Meerloo, Joost A. M. 1964. *Unobtrusive communication.* Assen, Netherlands: Van Gorcum.

Merriam, Alan P. 1964. *The anthropology of music.* Evanston, Il.: Northwestern.

Mills, M., and E. Melhuish. 1974. Recognition of mother's voice in early infancy. *Science* 252:123–24.

Moses, Paul. 1954. *The voice of neurosis.* New York: Grune & Stratton.

Murphy, M. 1983. Music therapy: A self-help group experience for substance abuse patients. *Music Therapy: The Journal of the American Association for Music Therapy* 3(1):52–62

Nordoff, P., and C. Robbins. 1977. *Creative music therapy.* New York: John Day.

Ostwald, Peter. 1973. Musical development in early childhood. *Developmental Medicine and Child Neurology* 15:367–75.

————. 1973. *The semiotics of human sound.* The Hague: Mouton & Co. N.V.

Pearce, Kathy A. 1981. Effects of different types of music on physical strength. *Perceptual and Motor Skills* 53:351–52.

Perls, Frederick, Ralph F. Hefferline, and Paul Goodman. 1951. *Gestalt therapy.* New York: Bantam.

Polster, Erving, and Miriam Polster. 1973. *Gestalt therapy integrated.* New York: Random House.

Reese, Sam. 1977. Forms of feeling: The aesthetic theory of Susanne K. Langer. *Music Educator's Journal* (April).

Reich, Wilhelm. 1973. *The function of the orgasm.* New York: Simon & Schuster.

Robbins, C., and C. Robbins. 1980. *Music for the hearing impaired.* St. Louis: Magnamusic Baton.

Rudhyar, Dane. 1979. *The rebirth of Hindu music.* New York: Samuel Weiser.

Salk, Lee. 1960. The effects of the normal heartbeat sound on the behavior of the newborn infant: Implications for mental health. *World Mental Health* 12:168–75.

Sanders, S. J., W. H. Tedford, and B. W. Hardy. 1977. Effects of musical stimuli on creativity. *Psychological Record* 2:463–71.

Schafer, Murray R. 1977. *The tuning of the world.* New York: Knopf.

Schmalz, Jeffrey. 1984. Sound Avant-Garde Fills Hartford Streets. *The New York Times* (July 7).

Shatin, Leo. 1970. Alteration of mood via music: A study of the vectoring effect. *Journal of Psychology* 75:81–86.

Smith, Carol A., and Larry W. Morris. Effects of stimulative and sedative music on cognitive and emotional components of anxiety. 1976. *Psychological Reports* 38:1187–1193.

————. Differential effects of stimulative and sedative music on anxiety, concentration and performance. 1977. *Psychological Reports* 41:1047–1053.

Steiner, Claude M. *Scripts people live.* 1974. New York: Bantam.

Spitz, René A. 1945. Hospitalism: An inquiry into the genesis of psychiatric conditions in early childhood. *Psychoanalytic Studies of the Child* 1:53–74.

Stanton, H. E. 1973. The effect of music on test anxiety. *Australian Psychologist* 8:220–28.

Stoudenmire, John. 1975. A comparison of muscle relaxation training and music in the reduction of state and trait anxiety. *Journal of Clinical Psychology* 31:490–92.

Trotter, Robert J. 1984. Maybe it's the music. *Psychology Today* (May):8.

Wallis, C. 1984. Unlocking pain's secrets. *Time* (June 11):66.

Wilson, Frank R. 1982. Mind, muscle, and music. *The American Music Teacher* 32(1).

Winston, Shirley Rabb. 1972. *Music as the bridge.* Va.: A.R.E. Press.

Wolfe, David E. 1978. Pain rehabilitation and music therapy. *Journal of Music Therapy* 25(4):162–78.

For Further Reading

Berne, Eric: 1961. *Transactional analysis in psychotherapy.* New York: Ballantine.

————. 1972. *What do you say after you say hello?* New York: Bantam.

Bright, Ruth. 1972. *Music in geriatric care.* New York: St. Martin's.

Chase, Mildred Portney. 1981. *Just being at the piano.* Ca.: Peace Press.

Meyer, Leonard. 1956. *Emotion and meaning in music.* Chicago: Univ. of Chicago.

Nordoff, Paul, and Clive Robbins. *Therapy in music for handicapped children.* 1971. New York: St. Martin's.

Priestly, Mary. 1975. *Music therapy in action.* London: Constable and Co.

Randolf, David. 1964. *This is music.* New York: Simon & Schuster.

Zinker, Joseph. 1977. *Creative process in Gestalt therapy.* New York: Random House.

Zuckerkandl, Victor. 1973. *Man the musician.* New Jersey: Princeton.

————. 1956. *Sound and symbol: Music and the external world.* New Jersey: Princeton.